★ ★ ★ ★ ★ ★

PRESIDENTIAL
TRIVIA

★ ★ ★ ★ ★ ★

REVISED AND UPDATED

ALSO BY RICHARD LEDERER

★ ★ ★ ★ ★ ★ ★

PRESIDENTIAL
TRIVIA

★ ★ ★ ★ ★ ★

THE FEATS, *FATES,*
FAMILIES, *FOIBLES,*
AND FIRSTS
OF OUR
AMERICAN
PRESIDENTS

★ ★ ★ ★ ★ ★

REVISED AND UPDATED

RICHARD LEDERER

GIBBS SMITH
TO ENRICH AND INSPIRE HUMANKIND

To Steve and Kathleen Flynn, great Americans

3rd Revised and Updated Edition
21 20 19 18 17   5 4 3 2 1

Text © 2007, 2009, 2017 Richard Lederer
See page 152 for image credits

Published by
Gibbs Smith
P.O. Box 667
Layton, Utah 84041

1.800.835.4993 orders
www.gibbs-smith.com

Designed by michelvrana.com and Virginia Snow
Printed and bound in Hong Kong

Gibbs Smith books are printed on paper produced from sustainable PEFC-certified forest/controlled wood source. Learn more at www.pefc.org.Library of Congress Cataloging-in-Publication Data

Names: Lederer, Richard, 1938- author.
Title: Presidential trivia : the feats, fates, families, foibles, and firsts
   of our American presidents / Richard Lederer.
Description: Revised third edition. | Layton, Utah : Gibbs Smith, 2017.
Identifiers: LCCN 2016045087 | ISBN 9781423646631 (pbk.)
Subjects: LCSH: Presidents--United States--History--Miscellanea. |
   Presidents--United States--Biography--Miscellanea.
Classification: LCC E176.1 .L335 2017 | DDC 973.09/9--dc23
LC record available at https://lccn.loc.gov/2016045087
ISBN: 978-1-4236-4663-1

Contents

Introduction

When George Washington became president in 1789, other national leaders included the king of France, the czarina of Russia, the emperor of China, and the shogun of Japan. Today, no king rules France, no czar rules Russia, no emperor rules China, and no shogun rules Japan. But the office of president of the United States endures and prevails. Very few nations have a governmental system that allows anyone to become the leader of the country; in this case, the most powerful in the world.

"When I was a boy I was told that anybody could become president; I'm beginning to believe it," quipped Clarence Darrow. It's true: Jefferson did it, Nixon did it, and Truman did it. So any Tom, Dick, and Harry can become president of the United States!

Our presidents have been highly educated and barely schooled: Woodrow Wilson earned a PhD in political science from Johns Hopkins University, while Andrew Johnson never attended school but was trained as a garment maker and wore only suits that he himself had custom tailored.

Our presidents have been filthy rich and dirt poor, generals and civilians, professional politicians and utter amateurs, sober as a judge and drunk as a skunk, eloquent and barely articulate, handsome and plug ugly. In the past half century, the White House has been occupied by a haberdasher, a schoolteacher, a peanut farmer, an actor, and the host of a television reality show.

Virginia, Ohio, New York, and Massachusetts have furnished most of our chief executives, but such widely scattered states as Vermont, Georgia, Tennessee, Missouri, Michigan, Iowa, and California have also sent native sons to the White House.

The framers of the Constitution could not have envisioned the power that the president now holds to influence world and domestic affairs. Our forefathers and foremothers could not have dreamt that presidents would be the subjects and objects of so much intense interest in their philosophies, opinions, policies, and personal lives.

Historian Henry Adams, the grandson and great-grandson of presidents, wrote that the president "resembles the commander of a ship at sea. He must have a helm to grasp, a course to steer, a port to seek." The voyages that our American presidents have steered on the ship of state are some of the brightest adventures that any nation has experienced since the dawn of civilization. To begin our exploration of our chief executives, let's review the names of the forty-four men (not forty-five; Grover Cleveland, for some bizarre reason, is traditionally counted twice) who have been president of the United States:

1. *George Washington, 1789–1797*
2. *John Adams, 1797–1801*
3. *Thomas Jefferson, 1801–1809*
4. *James Madison, 1809–1817*
5. *James Monroe, 1817–1825*
6. *John Quincy Adams, 1825–1829*
7. *Andrew Jackson, 1829–1837*
8. *Martin Van Buren, 1837–1841*
9. *William Henry Harrison, 1841*
10. *John Tyler, 1841–1845*
11. *James Knox Polk, 1845–1849*
12. *Zachary Taylor, 1849–1850*
13. *Millard Fillmore, 1850–1853*
14. *Franklin Pierce, 1853–1857*
15. *James Buchanan, 1857–1861*
16. *Abraham Lincoln, 1861–1865*
17. *Andrew Johnson, 1865–1869*
18. *Ulysses Simpson Grant, 1869–1877*
19. *Rutherford Birchard Hayes, 1877–1881*
20. *James Abram Garfield, 1881*
21. *Chester Alan Arthur, 1881–1885*
22. *Grover Cleveland, 1885–1889*
23. *Benjamin Harrison, 1889–1893*

24. *Grover Cleveland, 1893–1897*
25. *William McKinley, 1897–1901*
26. *Theodore Roosevelt, 1901–1909*
27. *William Howard Taft, 1909–1913*
28. *Woodrow Wilson, 1913–1921*
29. *Warren Gamaliel Harding, 1921–1923*
30. *Calvin Coolidge, 1923–1929*
31. *Herbert Clark Hoover, 1929–1933*
32. *Franklin Delano Roosevelt, 1933–1945*
33. *Harry S. Truman, 1945–1953*
34. *Dwight David Eisenhower 1953–1961*
35. *John Fitzgerald Kennedy, 1961–1963*
36. *Lyndon Baines Johnson, 1963–1969*
37. *Richard Milhous Nixon, 1969–1974*
38. *Gerald Rudolph Ford, 1974–1977*
39. *James Earl Carter, Jr., 1977–1981*
40. *Ronald Wilson Reagan, 1981–1989*
41. *George Herbert Walker Bush, 1989–1993*
42. *William Jefferson Clinton, 1993–2001*
43. *George Walker Bush, 2001–2009*
44. *Barack Hussein Obama, 2009–2017*
45. *Donald John Trump, 2017–*

PRESIDENTIAL
PRECEDENTS

★ ★ ★ ★

WHO WAS THE FIRST PRESIDENT BORN A UNITED STATES CITIZEN?

Martin Van Buren (1837–1841), our eighth president, entered the earthly stage on December 5, 1782, making him the first president born after the Declaration of Independence was signed. Eight presidents were born before 1776 as British subjects—**George Washington, John Adams, Thomas Jefferson, James Madison, James Monroe, John Quincy Adams, Andrew Jackson,** and, after Van Buren,

Martin Van Buren

William Henry Harrison. To put it another way, eight of our first nine presidents were not born in the United States; they were born in the American colonies.

WHO WAS THE FIRST PRESIDENT TO BE IMPEACHED?

If you answered **Richard Nixon,** you're mistaken. President Nixon resigned before any impeachment trial. **Andrew Johnson** and **Bill Clinton** were tried under the articles of impeachment. Both were acquitted (Johnson by a single vote in the Senate), but still, they were both impeached.

First and foremost, here's a quiz about presidential firsts. **Hint:** The answers to the questions are, for the most part, in the order of when each president served.

1 WHO WAS THE FIRST PRESIDENT TO APPEAR ON A POSTAGE STAMP?

The first official U.S. government adhesive postage stamps were issued on July 1, 1847. **George Washington** appeared on the ten-cent denomination.

2 THERE HAVE BEEN SIX PATCHES IN AMERICAN HISTORY WHEN NO FORMER PRESIDENT WAS ALIVE. WHO WAS THE FIRST PRESIDENT TO SERVE DURING YEARS WHEN NO FORMER PRESIDENT WAS ALIVE?

chuckle, chuckle, snort **George Washington.** There could be no former presidents alive during the term of our first president. The most recent president to fit this category was **Richard Nixon.** After **Lyndon Johnson** died on January 22, 1973, Nixon was president for more than a year and a half during which no former president was alive.

3 WHO WAS THE FIRST VICE PRESIDENT TO BECOME PRESIDENT?
Vice President **John Adams** succeeded **George Washington** as president.

4 WHO WAS THE FIRST U.S. CONGRESSMAN TO BECOME PRESIDENT?
Before he became our fourth president, **James Madison** was the youngest member of the Continental Congress.

5 WHO WAS THE FIRST PRESIDENT TO WEAR TROUSERS RATHER THAN KNEE BREECHES?
James Madison.

6 WHO WAS THE FIRST WARTIME PRESIDENT?
The War of 1812 raged during the administration of **James Madison.** In that conflict, the British torched Washington, DC.

7 WHO WAS THE FIRST PRESIDENT TO LIVE IN A WHITE HOUSE THAT WAS ACTUALLY WHITE?
When **James Monroe** began his presidency in 1817, the Executive Mansion was painted white. Before that, the building was gray.

8 WHO WAS THE FIRST CANDIDATE FOR THE DEMOCRATIC PARTY TO BE ELECTED PRESIDENT?
Andrew Jackson, in 1828.

9 WHO WAS THE FIRST PRESIDENT BORN IN A LOG CABIN?
Andrew Jackson (not **Abraham Lincoln**). Although several more have claimed it, there were only five others— **Millard Fillmore, James Buchanan, Abraham Lincoln, Andrew Johnson,** and **James Garfield.**

10 WHO WAS THE FIRST VICE PRESIDENT TO ASSUME THE PRESIDENCY BECAUSE OF THE DEATH OF THE PRESIDENT?

John Tyler, who succeeded **William Henry Harrison.** As a result, Tyler was nicknamed "His Accidency."

11 WHO WAS THE FIRST PRESIDENT TO SUFFER THE DEATH OF HIS WIFE WHILE IN OFFICE, AND THE FIRST TO MARRY DURING HIS PRESIDENCY?

John Tyler.

12 WHO WAS THE FIRST PRESIDENT TO BE PROTECTED BY A FEDERALLY FUNDED SECURITY FORCE?

John Tyler. The staff consisted of four men.

13 WHO WAS THE FIRST PRESIDENT FOR WHOM "HAIL TO THE CHIEF" WAS PLAYED WHENEVER HE APPEARED?

The tradition of playing "Hail to the Chief" whenever a president appeared at a state function was started by **John Tyler**'s second wife, Julia Gardiner.

14 WHO WAS THE FIRST "DARK-HORSE" CANDIDATE TO BECOME PRESIDENT?

James Polk, in 1844. The other dark-horse presidents were **Franklin Pierce** in 1852, **Rutherford B. Hayes** in 1876, **James Garfield** in 1880, and **Warren Harding** in 1920.

15 WHO WAS THE FIRST PRESIDENT TO RETIRE VOLUNTARILY AFTER ONE TERM?

James Polk.

John Tyler

★ PRESIDENTIAL PRECEDENTS ★

16 WHO WAS THE FIRST PRESIDENT BORN IN THE NINETEENTH CENTURY?

Entering the earthly stage in 1804, **Franklin Pierce** was the first president born in the nineteenth century.

17 WHO WAS THE FIRST CANDIDATE FOR THE REPUBLICAN PARTY TO BE ELECTED PRESIDENT?

Abraham Lincoln, in 1860.

18 WHO WAS THE FIRST PRESIDENT BORN OUTSIDE OF THE ORIGINAL THIRTEEN COLONIES?

Abraham Lincoln began life in Hodgenville, Kentucky. Many believe incorrectly that he was born in Illinois, but our only president who started life in Illinois was **Ronald Reagan,** born in Tampico.

19 WHO WAS THE FIRST PRESIDENT TO WEAR A BEARD?

Abraham Lincoln was our first bearded president. Some say he was simply responding to a letter from an eleven-year-old girl, Grace Bedell, who

suggested that a beard would improve his appearance. **Benjamin Harrison** was the last bearded president, and the mustachioed **William Howard Taft** the last to sport facial hair. **William McKinley** was the only clean-shaven president between **Andrew Johnson** and **Woodrow Wilson.**

20 WHO WAS THE FIRST PRESIDENT TO BE ASSASSINATED?

Abraham Lincoln. Five days after the end of the Civil War, on April 14, 1865, he was fatally shot by the actor John Wilkes Booth. Three more presidents have been assassinated while in office— **James Garfield, William McKinley,** and **John F. Kennedy.**

Geyser at Yellowstone National Park

21 WHO WAS THE FIRST PRESIDENT TO ESTABLISH A NATIONAL PARK?

Ulysses S. Grant established Yellowstone as the nation's first national park on March 1, 1872. **Theodore Roosevelt** is the only president to have a national park named after him. The park, in North Dakota, contains part of Roosevelt's ranch. In 1936, **Gerald Ford** served as a park ranger in Yellowstone, the only president who was employed by the National Park Service.

22 WHO WAS THE FIRST PRESIDENT TO HAVE ELECTRIC LIGHTS AT THE WHITE HOUSE?

Benjamin Harrison. After Harrison received an electric shock, his family was scared to death to use the light switches.

23 WHO WAS THE FIRST PRESIDENT TO ATTEND A BASEBALL GAME?

Benjamin Harrison. He saw the Cincinnati Reds beat the Washington Senators 7–4 on June 6, 1892.

24 **WHO WAS THE FIRST PRESIDENT TO RIDE IN AN AUTOMOBILE?**
William McKinley. In 1901 an ambulance transported him from the Pan-American Exposition in Buffalo, where he was shot, to the home where his wife and he were staying. **William Howard Taft** was the first president to own an automobile. He had the White House stables converted to a four-car garage, which housed, among other vehicles, Baker Electric cars. That's right, some of the first automobiles in America were electric.

25 **WHO WAS THE FIRST PRESIDENT TO OFFICIALLY REFER TO THE EXECUTIVE MANSION AS THE WHITE HOUSE?**
Theodore Roosevelt declared by presidential proclamation that the Executive Mansion should henceforth be known as the "White House," and was the first to use that term on presidential stationery.

26 **WHO WAS THE FIRST PRESIDENT TO FLY IN AN AIRPLANE?**

On October 11, 1910, **Theodore Roosevelt** took a four-minute flight in a plane built by the Wright Brothers. The next Roosevelt—**Franklin Roosevelt**—was the first president to have a presidential aircraft.

27 **WHO WAS THE FIRST PRESIDENT TO TRAVEL ABROAD DURING HIS ADMINISTRATION?**
Theodore Roosevelt visited Panama in 1906 during his second term. He was also the first president to visit every state. The first U.S. president to visit a European country while serving as president was **Woodrow Wilson,** who arrived at Brest, France, on December 13, 1918.

28 **WHO WAS THE FIRST PRESIDENT TO WIN A NOBEL PRIZE?**
Theodore Roosevelt won the Nobel Peace Prize in 1906 for mediating the Russo-Japanese War Treaty. **Woodrow Wilson, Jimmy Carter,** and **Barack Obama** were also accorded that honor.

Woodrow Wilson throwing out first pitch, 1916

In 1920, the handsome **Warren G. Harding** won a landslide 60 percent of the popular vote, helped by women voting for the first time.

29 WHO WAS THE FIRST PRESIDENT TO THROW OUT THE "FIRST PITCH" OF THE BASEBALL SEASON?

William Howard Taft threw out the first pitch on April 4, 1910, during an opening-day game between the Washington Senators and the Philadelphia Athletics. Since Taft's first pitch, every president but one, **Jimmy Carter,** has opened at least one baseball season during their tenure.

30 WHO WAS THE FIRST PRESIDENT IN WHOSE ELECTION WOMEN WERE ALLOWED TO VOTE?

31 WHO WAS THE FIRST SITTING SENATOR TO BE ELECTED PRESIDENT?

Warren Harding was the first seated senator to win the presidency, followed only by **John F. Kennedy** and **Barack Obama.**

32 WHO WAS THE FIRST PRESIDENT BORN WEST OF THE MISSISSIPPI RIVER?

Herbert Hoover was the first president born west of the Mississippi. His birthplace is the village of West Branch, Iowa.

33 WHO WAS THE FIRST PRESIDENT TO APPROVE "THE STAR-SPANGLED BANNER" AS OUR NATIONAL ANTHEM?

On March 3, 1931, **Herbert Hoover** signed into law a congressional act designating "The Star-Spangled Banner" as our official national anthem.

34 WHO WAS THE FIRST PRESIDENT WHOSE MOTHER WAS ELIGIBLE TO VOTE FOR HIM?

Franklin Roosevelt was the first president whose mother (Sara Ann Delano Roosevelt) was eligible and alive to cast a ballot for her son. By the way, she made him wear dresses for the first five years of his life.

35 WHO WAS THE FIRST PRESIDENT TO APPOINT A WOMAN TO HIS CABINET?

Franklin Roosevelt appointed the first woman to the cabinet—Frances Perkins. She became the secretary of labor. Perkins fought to establish a minimum wage, overtime pay, the forty-hour workweek, and the end of child labor.

36 UNDER WHICH PRESIDENT WAS THE USO (UNITED SERVICE ORGANIZATIONS) ESTABLISHED?

In 1941, **Franklin Roosevelt** approved the creation of the USO as a private, nonprofit institution.

37 WHICH PRESIDENT BEGAN THE TRADITION OF THE PRESIDENTIAL LIBRARY?

Franklin Roosevelt started the presidential library tradition in 1939, when he donated his papers to the United States and asked the National Archives to administer them. His presidential library in Hyde Park, New York, was the first to be dedicated.

38

WHO WAS THE FIRST PRESIDENT TO ASSUME OFFICE DURING WARTIME?

Harry Truman was the first president to take office during wartime, succeeding **Franklin Roosevelt** toward the end of World War II.

39

WHO WAS THE FIRST PRESIDENT OF ALL FIFTY STATES?

Hawaii became our fiftieth state on August 21, 1959, during the second half of **Dwight Eisenhower**'s second term.

40

WHO WAS THE FIRST PRESIDENT TO EARN A PILOT'S LICENSE?

Dwight Eisenhower, in 1939.

41

WHO WAS THE FIRST PRESI-DENT BORN IN THE TWENTIETH CENTURY?

Born in Brookline, Massachusetts, on May 29, 1917, **John F. Kennedy** was the first man born in the twentieth century to serve as president. **Lyndon Johnson, Richard Nixon, Gerald Ford,** and **Ronald Reagan** were all born before JFK in the twentieth century but served after him.

42

WHO WAS THE FIRST PRESIDENT TO HAVE SERVED IN THE U.S. NAVY?

Lt. John F. Kennedy, 1942

If the army was the most common branch of military service for earlier presidents, the navy attracted the greatest number of presidents who served in the second half of the twentieth century. **John F. Kennedy** was the first president to have served in the U.S. Navy, followed by **Lyndon Johnson, Richard Nixon, Gerald Ford, Jimmy Carter,** and **George H. W. Bush.**

43 WHO WAS THE FIRST PRESIDENT TO NAME AN AFRICAN AMERICAN TO HIS CABINET?

Lyndon Johnson, who chose Robert Weaver to head the new Department of Housing and Urban Development.

44 WHO WAS THE FIRST PRESIDENT TO APPOINT AN AFRICAN AMERICAN TO THE SUPREME COURT?

Lyndon Johnson appointed Thurgood Marshall as a justice of the Supreme Court. **George H. W. Bush** appointed the second African American justice, Clarence Thomas.

Thurgood Marshall

45 WHO WAS THE FIRST PRESIDENT TO VISIT ALL FIFTY STATES?

Richard Nixon.

46 WHO WAS THE FIRST PRESIDENT TO VISIT THE SOVIET UNION AND MAINLAND CHINA?

Richard Nixon.

47 **WHO WAS THE FIRST PRESIDENT FOR WHOM EIGHTEEN-YEAR-OLDS COULD VOTE?**

The Twenty-Sixth Amendment to the Constitution, ratified by a majority of the states in 1971, during **Richard Nixon**'s first term, granted suffrage to eighteen-year-olds.

48 **WHO WAS THE FIRST PRESIDENT BORN IN A HOSPITAL?**

Jimmy Carter, in 1924. All previous presidents were born at home.

49 **WHO WAS THE FIRST BABY BOOMER TO BE ELECTED PRESIDENT?**

Born August 19, 1946, **Bill Clinton** was the first baby boomer to be elected president and the first born after World War II. Born July 6, 1946, **George W. Bush** was the second presidential boomer, followed by **Barack Obama,** born on August 4, 1961, and **Donald Trump,** born June 14, 1946. That makes 1946 the only year in which three presidents were born (and within three months of each other).

50 **WHO WAS THE FIRST PRESIDENT NOT TO HAVE HAD PREVIOUS EXPERIENCE AS PRESIDENT, VICE PRESIDENT, GOVERNOR, MEMBER OF CONGRESS, CABINET MEMBER, OR GENERAL?**

Donald Trump. Since the start of the twentieth century, only four men have become president without having held major elective office—**William Howard Taft, Herbert Hoover, Dwight Eisenhower,** and **Donald Trump.** But the first three previously occupied at least one of the positions described above.

Bill Clinton

ONE AND ONLY
PRESIDENTS

WHO WAS THE ONLY PRESIDENT WHO DID NOT SERVE IN WASHINGTON, DC?

The only president who didn't live in Washington was . . . Washington. During **George Washington**'s administration the nation's capital was located in Philadelphia. It was **John Adams** who first occupied what was then known as the President's House, on 1600 Pennsylvania Avenue. The Adams family moved into the President's House on November 1, 1800, while the paint was still drying. During the move, the family got lost for several hours in the woods north of Washington, DC. Adams occupied the President's House for only four months, having lived most of his term in Philadelphia.

President's House, 1807

WHO WAS THE ONLY PRESIDENT TO BE UNANIMOUSLY ELECTED?

George Washington was the only president to be unanimously elected by the Electoral College, and he did it twice. In 1820, incumbent **James Monroe** won all the electoral votes except one. The "faithless elector" who voted against him was a New Hampshire delegate who felt strongly that only Washington should have the historical honor of being elected president unanimously.

Our first and fifth presidents are connected in other ways: **George Washington** (both terms) and **James Monroe** (second term) were the only two presidents to run unopposed. Washington and Monroe are also our only two presidents who had national capitals named after them—Washington, DC, and Monrovia, the capital of Liberia.

Washington is the only president after whom a state is named, while four state capitals commemorate four other presidents—Jefferson City, Missouri; Madison, Wisconsin; Jackson, Mississippi; and Lincoln, Nebraska.

WHO WAS THE ONLY PRESIDENT TO RUN AS THE CANDIDATE OF A MAJOR PARTY IN A PRESIDENTIAL ELECTION AND COME OUT THIRD?

In 1912, President **William Howard Taft** ran as a Republican for reelection against the Democratic nominee, **Woodrow Wilson.** Former president **Theodore Roosevelt** said of Taft, "Taft meant well, but he meant well feebly," so Roosevelt also entered the presidential fray, as a candidate for the Bull Moose Party.

Roosevelt and Taft split the Republican vote, and Wilson won handily, garnering 42 percent of the popular vote, with 27 percent going to TR, the best showing ever by a third-party candidate. Taft

William Howard Taft

Try your hand and brain at a quiz about presidential onlys:

1 WHO WAS THE ONLY PRESIDENT WHO DID NOT REPRESENT A POLITICAL PARTY WHEN HE WAS FIRST ELECTED?
George Washington was not a member of a political party when he was elected to his first term.

2 WHO WERE THE ONLY PRESIDENTS TO SIGN THE DECLARATION OF INDEPENDENCE?
John Adams and Thomas Jefferson.

3 WHO WERE THE ONLY PRESIDENTS TO SIGN THE CONSTITUTION?
George Washington and James Madison.

4 WHO WAS THE ONLY PRESIDENT TO BE DEFEATED BY HIS VICE PRESIDENT?
In 1801, Vice President **Thomas Jefferson** defeated his president, **John Adams,** the only president to experience that turnabout.

placed third with an abysmal 23 percent of the vote, the lowest ever for an incumbent president. Unremittingly good humored, Taft sighed, "I have one consolation. No one candidate was ever elected ex-president by such a large majority."

5 **WHO WAS THE ONLY PRESIDENT TO FOUND A UNIVERSITY?**

Thomas Jefferson founded the University of Virginia in 1819. Before they became U.S. presidents, **James Garfield** was president of Hiram College, **Woodrow Wilson** was president of Princeton University, and **Dwight Eisenhower** president of Columbia University.

6 **WHO WAS THE ONLY PRESIDENT TO HAVE SERVED IN TWO DIFFERENT CABINET POSTS?**

James Monroe served as secretary of state and secretary of war, the only president to do so.

7 **WHO WAS THE ONLY PRESIDENT TO SERVE IN THE HOUSE OF REPRESENTATIVES AFTER HIS PRESIDENCY?**

John Quincy Adams labored in the House of Representatives for seventeen years, where he accomplished more in that time than he did as president. He remains the only president to serve in the House after his presidential term ended. In 1848, he suffered a fatal

Thomas Jefferson

cerebral stroke and fell to the floor of the House of Representatives. Missouri Senator Thomas Hart Benton eulogized, "Where else could death have found him but at the post of duty?"

8 **WHO WAS THE ONLY PRESIDENT TO HAVE SERVED IN BOTH THE AMERICAN REVOLUTION AND THE WAR OF 1812?**

Andrew Jackson was the only president to serve in both conflicts. He was also the only president to have been a prisoner of war, captured during the Revolution at the age of thirteen.

9 WHO WAS THE ONLY PRESIDENT FOR WHOM ENGLISH WAS A SECOND LANGUAGE?

Martin Van Buren was the first president of Dutch ancestry. He grew up speaking Dutch, and his wife and he spoke Dutch at home.

10 WHO WAS THE ONLY PRESIDENT WHO WAS THE GRANDFATHER OF ANOTHER PRESIDENT?

William Henry Harrison was grandfather to **Benjamin Harrison,** one of his forty-eight (!) grandchildren. The younger Harrison was named after his great-grandfather, a signer of the Declaration of Independence.

William Henry Harrison

Benjamin Harrison

11 WHO WERE THE ONLY TWO PRESIDENTS WHO DIED IN THE WHITE HOUSE?

William Henry Harrison in 1841 and **Zachary Taylor** in 1850 were our only two presidents who shuffled off their mortal coil in the White House itself.

12 WHO WAS THE ONLY PRESIDENT NAMED A SWORN ENEMY OF THE UNITED STATES?

John Tyler joined the Confederacy twenty years after he was in office and became the only president named a sworn enemy of the United States. He was also the only president who was not a U.S. citizen when he died, in Virginia, as a citizen of the Confederate States of America. At his request, his coffin was draped with a Confederate flag.

13 WHO WAS THE ONLY PRESIDENT TO HAVE BEEN SPEAKER OF THE HOUSE OF REPRESENTATIVES?

James Polk.

14 AMONG PRESIDENTS WHO SERVED FOR AT LEAST ONE FULL TERM, WHO WAS THE ONLY ONE WHO HAD NO TURNOVER IN HIS CABINET?

There were no cabinet changes during the four years (1853–1857) that **Franklin Pierce** served as president, the only time that has happened during a full presidential term.

Franklin Pierce

15 **WHO WAS THE ONLY PRESIDENT WHOSE PARTY REFUSED TO NOMINATE HIM FOR A SECOND TERM?**
Franklin Pierce. During Pierce's term as president, his own party adopted the campaign slogan "Anybody but Pierce." No surprise, then, that Pierce decided not to run for reelection. **James Buchanan** was nominated as an alternative to Pierce and won the endorsement on the seventeenth ballot.

16 **WHO WAS THE ONLY PRESIDENT TO BE THE FATHER-IN-LAW OF ANOTHER PRESIDENT?**
Zachary Taylor was the father-in-law of Jefferson Davis, president of the Confederacy. Three months after eloping with Davis, Taylor's daughter Sarah died.

17 **WHO WAS THE ONLY PRESIDENT NEVER TO MARRY?**
James Buchanan was known as the Bachelor President. During his term in office, his niece, Harriet Lane, played the role of First Lady. In 1819, Buchanan became engaged to Anne Coleman, daughter of the richest man in Pennsylvania. Through a misunderstanding their engagement was broken off. When Anne died mysteriously a short time later, Buchanan vowed he would never marry. **Grover Cleveland** also entered the White House as a bachelor, but married while he was president.

18 **WHO WAS THE ONLY PRESIDENT TO BE AWARDED A PATENT?**
Abraham Lincoln. He was awarded a patent for a system of buoying vessels over shoals.

19 **WHO WAS THE ONLY PRESIDENT TO SERVE IN THE SENATE AFTER HIS PRESIDENCY?**
Andrew Johnson is the only former president elected to the U.S. Senate, the very body that almost kicked him out of office. His triumphant return to that body was short lived. In less than four months he died of a stroke.

20 WHO WAS THE ONLY PRESIDENT TO HAVE BEEN A PREACHER?

James Garfield.

James Garfield

21 WHO WAS THE ONLY PRESIDENT TO HAVE HANGED PEOPLE?

When he was sheriff of Erie County, New York, **Grover Cleveland** placed the noose around the neck of two convicted criminals, the only American president to have personally hanged anyone.

22 WHO WAS THE ONLY PRESIDENT TO BE MARRIED IN THE WHITE HOUSE?

Grover Cleveland, who, at the age of forty-nine, married twenty-one-year-old Frances Folsom in the Blue Room of the White House. Their baby, Ruth, was the first child born in the White House.

23 WHO WAS THE ONLY PRESIDENT TO SERVE TWO NONCONSECUTIVE TERMS?

Grover Cleveland was both our twenty-second and twenty-fourth president, forever confusing the mathematics of the presidential sequence.

24 WHO WAS THE ONLY PRESIDENT TO SERVE AS A SUPREME COURT JUSTICE AFTER HIS PRESIDENCY?

When **William Howard Taft** was appointed chief justice of the Supreme Court eight years after his presidency, he became the only man ever to have headed both the executive and judicial branches of our government.

25 WHO WAS THE ONLY PRESIDENT TO DEFEAT TWO CHIEF JUSTICES OF THE SUPREME COURT?

In the election of 1912, **Woodrow Wilson** defeated **William Howard Taft,** who went on to become chief justice of the Supreme Court in 1921. In the next election, 1916, Wilson defeated Charles Evans Hughes, who succeeded Taft as chief justice of the Supreme Court in 1930.

26 WHO IS THE ONLY PRESIDENT BURIED IN WASHINGTON, DC?

Woodrow Wilson is the only president interred in Washington, DC. He is buried at the Washington National Cathedral. Wilson was also the only former president to retire to Washington, DC.

27 WHO WERE OUR ONLY QUAKER PRESIDENTS?

Herbert Hoover and **Richard Nixon** are our only presidents who were Quakers. They were eighth cousins once removed.

William Howard Taft as chief justice

28 WHO WAS THE ONLY PRESIDENT AFTER WHOM TWO ASTEROIDS HAVE BEEN NAMED?

The asteroids Herbert and Hoover were named in honor of **Herbert Hoover.** Less happily, the Hoovervilles, shantytowns of temporary dwellings that sprang up during the Great Depression, were also named for President Hoover, as were Hoover wagons (broken-down automobiles), Hoover blankets (newspapers used as blankets by the homeless), and Hoover flags (empty pockets turned inside out to show the penury of their owners). The asteroids Washingtonia, Quincy, Lincoln, and Grant have also been named for U.S. presidents.

29 WHO WAS THE ONLY TWENTIETH-CENTURY PRESIDENT WHO DIDN'T ATTEND COLLEGE?
Nine presidents never attended college, but only one of them served in the last century: **Harry Truman.**

30 WHO WAS THE ONLY PRESIDENT WITH MILITARY SERVICE IN BOTH WORLD WARS?
Dwight Eisenhower served as a major in World War I and General of the Army in World War II. Twelve presidents were generals, but Eisenhower was the only one in the twentieth century. In 1976, **Gerald Ford** posthumously promoted **George Washington** to "General of the Armies of the United

States," a rank forever above all other officers of the U.S. Army.

31 WHO WAS THE ONLY BALD PRESIDENT OF THE TWENTIETH CENTURY?
While **John Adams, John Quincy Adams, Martin Van Buren,** and **James Garfield** were folliclularly challenged among nineteenth-century presidents, **Dwight Eisenhower** was the only bald

Dwight Eisenhower

president of the last century. If you consider **Gerald Ford** to have become bald (I don't), then Eisenhower is the only bald president *elected* during the twentieth century. More subjectively, among all our presidents, **Andrew Jackson, John F. Kennedy, Ronald Reagan,** and **Bill Clinton** sported the most luxurious heads of hair.

32 WHO WAS THE ONLY ROMAN CATHOLIC PRESIDENT?

John F. Kennedy was the only Roman Catholic president. An earlier Catholic nominee for president, Al Smith, was soundly defeated by **Herbert Hoover** in 1928.

33 WHO WAS THE ONLY PRESIDENT TO APPOINT HIS BROTHER TO A CABINET POST?

John F. Kennedy appointed his brother, Robert Kennedy, to the post of attorney general.

34 WHO WAS THE ONLY PRESIDENT TO BE SURVIVED BY BOTH HIS PARENTS?

Assassinated at age forty-six, **John F. Kennedy** is the only president whose parents both outlived him.

35 WHO WAS THE ONLY PRESIDENT TO BE PRESENT AT HIS PREDECESSOR'S ASSASSINATION?

Lyndon Johnson was in Dallas when **John F. Kennedy** was assassinated on November 22, 1963.

36 WHO WAS THE ONLY PRESIDENT TO RESIGN FROM OFFICE?

Richard Nixon resigned from the White House on August 9, 1974, the only president to do so. Spiro Agnew, his vice president, had resigned earlier.

Brothers Robert, Ted, and John F. Kennedy

37 WHO WAS THE ONLY MAN TO BE PRESIDENT AND VICE PRESIDENT BUT NOT ELECTED TO EITHER OFFICE?

As a result of the events described above, **Gerald Ford,** for two years, was the only man who served as both vice president (replacing Agnew) and president (replacing Nixon) without having been elected to either office. Ford was our only president never elected to national office. The only elected office he ever held was a western Michigan congressional seat. Ford's vice president, Nelson Rockefeller, was also not elected to his office.

38 WHO WAS THE ONLY PRESIDENT TO GRADUATE FROM THE U.S. NAVAL ACADEMY?

The only president to graduate from the U.S. Naval Academy was **Jimmy Carter,** in the class of 1946. **Ulysses S. Grant** and **Dwight Eisenhower** were the only presidents to have graduated from the U.S. Military Academy at West Point.

U.S. Naval Academy, Annapolis, Maryland

39 WHO WAS THE ONLY PRESIDENT TO HAVE OFFICIALLY REPORTED A UFO SIGHTING?

Jimmy Carter officially reported a sighting to the International UFO Bureau, the only president to have done so. He described a noiseless object "as bright as the moon" that came within 900 yards of his party.

40 WHO WAS THE ONLY PRESIDENT TO BECOME AN EAGLE SCOUT?

Gerald Ford was the only president to have attained the rank of Eagle Scout. Scouting was so important to Ford that his family asked that scouts participate in his funeral. Four hundred Eagle Scouts, ages fifteen to eighty-five, lined the road to his Grand Rapids, Michigan, presidential museum. They

were there to welcome home the only Eagle Scout to serve as president of the United States.

41 WHO WERE THE ONLY TWO PRESIDENTS WHO HAD A CAREER IN MODELING?

Gerald Ford appeared in a *Look* magazine pictorial and on the cover of *Cosmopolitan* magazine. **Ronald Reagan** modeled for Arrow shirts, among other products.

42 WHO ARE THE ONLY TWO PRESIDENTS TO HAVE BEEN DIVORCED?

Ronald Reagan was our first divorced president. He had been married to the actress Jane Wyman. **Donald Trump** divorced two wives, Ivana Zelníčková and Marla Maples.

43 WHO WAS THE ONLY PRESIDENT TO HAVE HEADED A LABOR UNION?

Ronald Reagan was president of the Screen Actors Guild. While a labor union leader, conservative standard bearer Reagan once voted for a Democratic president; he cast his ballot for New Dealer **Franklin Roosevelt.**

44 WHO WAS THE ONLY PRESIDENT TO HAVE BEEN DIRECTOR OF THE CIA?

George H. W. Bush, who was also the only president to have been chairman of his political party and ambassador to the United Nations.

45 WHO WAS THE ONLY PRESIDENT TO HAVE BEEN A RHODES SCHOLAR?

Bill Clinton graduated from Georgetown University, and in 1968 won a Rhodes Scholarship to Oxford University, the only president to do so.

46 WHO WAS THE ONLY DEMOCRATIC PRESIDENT TO WIN REELECTION DURING THE SECOND HALF OF THE TWENTIETH CENTURY?

In 1996, **Bill Clinton** became the only Democratic president since **Franklin Roosevelt** to win reelection, a span of more than fifty years.

47 WHO WAS THE ONLY PRESIDENT ELECTED TWICE WITHOUT RECEIVING AT LEAST 50 PERCENT OF THE POPULAR VOTE EITHER TIME?

Bill Clinton received 43 percent of the popular vote in 1992 and 49 percent in 1996, the only president to fall short of 50 percent twice.

George W. Bush

48 WHO WAS THE ONLY PRESIDENT TO HAVE EARNED AN MBA (MASTER OF BUSINESS ADMINISTRATION)?

George W. Bush earned an MBA from the Harvard Business School, the only president with that degree.

49 WHO WAS THE ONLY PRESIDENT TO HAVE BEEN AN OWNER OF A MAJOR LEAGUE BASEBALL TEAM?

George W. Bush was the only owner of a major league baseball team to become president. (He was managing general partner of the Texas Rangers.)

50 WHO WAS THE ONLY PRESIDENT TO HAVE HAD A POLYGAMOUS GRANDFATHER?

Barack Obama's paternal grandfather, Hussein Onyango Obama, was a polygamist, married to at least four wives.

PRESIDENTIAL
RECORD
SETTERS

★ ★ ★ ★

CAN YOU NAME THE YOUNGEST MAN EVER TO HAVE SERVED AS PRESIDENT OF THE UNITED STATES?

If your answer is **John Fitzgerald Kennedy,** you're not quite correct. Kennedy was, at the age of forty-three, the youngest man ever to have been *elected* president, but **Theodore Roosevelt** became president at forty-two, when **William McKinley** was assassinated. When TR's second term was over, he was still only fifty years old, making him the youngest ex-president.

Theodore Roosevelt as a colonel in the Rough Riders

WHICH OF OUR PRESIDENTS APPOINTED THE GREATEST NUMBER OF SUPREME COURT JUSTICES?

The answer—of course—is **George Washington.** *chuckle, chuckle, snort again* During his two terms he appointed eleven justices. The number of Supreme Court justices has changed over the years, ranging from six at the outset to ten. President **Franklin Roosevelt** tried to increase the court to fifteen members, but the number has remained nine since 1869.

Now cast your ballot for a quiz about presidential mosts.

1 NOW THAT YOU KNOW THE IDENTITY OF OUR YOUNGEST PRESIDENT, WHO WAS OUR OLDEST PRESIDENT?
The average age at which America's presidents have taken office is fifty-four. In 2017, **Donald Trump** entered the Oval Office at the age of seventy years and seven months, exceeding the age of Ronald Reagan, who became president at sixty-nine years and eleven months. Before Reagan, **Dwight Eisenhower** had been the only president to reach the age of seventy while in office, and that was during the final ten months of his second term. **William Henry Harrison** attained the position at the age of sixty-eight but died only a month later. By Election Day of 2016, the combined ages of **Donald Trump** (seventy) and his opponent, Hillary Clinton (sixty-nine), by far exceeded the total of any other pair of major-party candidates for the presidency.

2 WHAT PRESIDENT LIVED THE LONGEST?
When **Ronald Reagan** died at the age of ninety-three years, 120 days, he was our longest-lived president. But on November 12, 2006, **Gerald Ford** surpassed that record and lived another month and a half. As of the publication of this book, both **George H. W. Bush** and **Jimmy Carter** have turned ninety-two. Amazingly, our fifth longest-lived president is **John Adams,** who was

born in 1735, lived for ninety years and eight months, and held the presidential longevity record for a century and three-quarters. Although the lifespan of Americans born in the eighteenth century was less than forty years, our first ten presidents lived an average of more than seventy-seven years. Twenty-three of the thirty-four presidents who have died of natural causes have exceeded the life expectancy of men the same age as when they were elected.

3 WHAT MAN SPENT THE GREATEST NUMBER OF YEARS AS A FORMER PRESIDENT?

In 2012, **Jimmy Carter** surpassed **Herbert Hoover**'s previous record of thirty-one years, seven months, and seventeen days as an ex-president.

4 WHAT PRESIDENT SPENT THE SHORTEST PERIOD AS A FORMER PRESIDENT?

James Polk proclaimed, "No president who performs his duties faithfully and conscientiously can have any leisure." He meant it: during Polk's four years in

James Polk

office, his wife Sara and he spent only six weeks away from the job. Over that span, no dancing, singing, or alcohol was permitted in the White House. He died just three months into his retirement, quite possibly from exhaustion.

5 WHAT PRESIDENT LIVED THE SHORTEST NUMBER OF YEARS?

John F. Kennedy took office at the age of forty-three, and after two-and-a-half years was assassinated at the age of forty-six. **James Polk** was our shortest-lived president to die out of office, at age fifty-three.

6 WHO WAS OUR TALLEST PRESIDENT?

Abraham Lincoln, at 6 feet 4 inches, was our loftiest president, at a time when the average Civil War soldier was 5 feet 7 inches. To the inevitable question, "How tall are you?" Lincoln would reply, "Tall enough to reach the ground." **Lyndon Johnson** reached the second-greatest height at 6 feet 3 1/2 inches. **George Washington, Thomas Jefferson,** and **Bill Clinton** measured up in third place at 6 feet 2 1/2 inches. Like our population, the average height of presidents has grown taller and is currently 5 feet 10 inches, although some of our tallest presidents came early. Almost all our presidents were taller than the average American living contemporaneously, and two-thirds of them have been taller than their closest opponent.

James Madison

7 WHO WAS OUR SHORTEST PRESIDENT?

James Madison, at 5 feet 4 inches and weighing about a hundred pounds, was our most compact president. Madison may be our only president who weighed less than his IQ. The author Washington Irving described him as "but a withered little apple-John," but another notable observer marveled that he had "never seen so much mind in so little matter." Yet another observer commented that when Thomas Jefferson and Madison went walking, the two looked "as if they were on their way to a father-son banquet." Tied for second place, at 5 feet 6 inches, are **Martin Van Buren** and **Benjamin Harrison.**

8 WHO WAS OUR FATTEST PRESIDENT?

William Howard Taft, at 6 feet and 300 to 340 pounds, was our fullest-figured president. A widely circulated story of disputed authenticity is that when he became stuck in the White House bathtub, Taft ordered a new one installed that would accommodate four men of average stature. Although Taft was the most portly president, he was considered a good dancer, a good tennis player, and a decent golfer. **Grover Cleveland,** at 5 feet 10 inches and 260 pounds, held the weighty record before Taft. Cleveland, sometimes called "the buxom Buffalonian," confessed that he was helpless in the presence of sausage, corned beef and cabbage, and thick-foamed German beer.

9 WHAT PRESIDENT HAD THE BIGGEST FEET?

Among U.S. presidents, **Warren G. Harding** had the largest feet: size 14. **George Washington, Abraham Lincoln,** and **Bill Clinton** each wore a size 13 boot and shoe.

10 WHO WAS PRESIDENT FOR THE SHORTEST PERIOD OF TIME?

William Howard Taft

William Henry Harrison died on the thirty-first day of his presidency. As a result, 1841 was a year in which three American presidents served—**Martin Van Buren,** Harrison, and **John Tyler.** Forty years later, in 1881, **James Garfield** was assassinated and held office for only 199 days. As a result, **Rutherford B. Hayes,** Garfield, and **Chester Arthur** all served that same year. The next three shortest terms were served by **Zachary Taylor** (one year, 127 days), **Warren Harding** (two years, 151 days—the shortest term in the twentieth century), and **Gerald Ford** (two years, 164 days). Ford is the only short-term president who did not die in office.

Warren Harding

11 WHO WAS PRESIDENT FOR THE LONGEST PERIOD OF TIME?

Franklin Roosevelt was elected to four terms as president and served from 1933 to 1945. This record can't be broken as long as the Twenty-Second Amendment, setting a limit of two terms, remains in effect. The exact wording is: "No person shall be elected to the office of the President more than twice, and no person who has held the office of President, or acted as President, for more than two years of a term to which some other person was elected President shall be elected to the office of the President more than once."

12 WHAT PRESIDENT HAD THE GREATEST NUMBER OF CHILDREN?

John Tyler was the most fatherly of presidents. He had three sons and five daughters with his first wife and five sons and two daughters with his second, for a total of fifteen offspring. From a single marriage, **William Henry Harrison** was the father of ten children—four girls and six boys, one of whom became the father of another president, **Benjamin Harrison.** Hence, the Harrison-Tyler ticket of 1840 was the most prolific in American history—engendering a total of twenty-five children!

13 WHAT PRESIDENT WAS OUR MOST DEVOTED BIBLE READER?

John Quincy Adams annually read the Bible cover to cover.

14 WHAT PRESIDENT RAN IN THE GREATEST NUMBER OF PRESIDENTIAL AND VICE PRESIDENTIAL ELECTIONS AS A REPUBLICAN?

Richard Nixon ran successfully as a Republican candidate for the office of vice president in 1952 and 1956, unsuccessfully for president in 1960, and successfully for president in 1968 and 1972. Total: five.

15 WHAT PRESIDENT RAN IN THE GREATEST NUMBER OF PRESIDENTIAL AND VICE PRESIDENTIAL ELECTIONS AS A DEMOCRAT?

Franklin Roosevelt ran unsuccessfully as a Democratic candidate for the office of vice president in 1920 and successfully for president in 1932, 1936, 1940, and 1944. Total: five.

16 WHO WAS OUR MOST TRAVELED PRESIDENT?

Bill Clinton set a record for the most trips abroad: 133.

17 WHICH PRESIDENT WON THE LARGEST PERCENTAGE OF THE POPULAR VOTE (SINCE THAT FIGURE BEGAN TO BE TABULATED IN 1824)?

In 1964, **Lyndon Johnson** defeated Barry Goldwater by a margin of 16 million votes and with 61.1 percent of the popular vote, the largest percentage ever recorded. **Franklin Roosevelt**'s 523–8 Electoral College victory over Alfred M. Landon in 1936 was the largest electoral

Franklin D. Roosevelt

landslide since **James Monroe** won all but a single Electoral College vote. In 1984, **Ronald Reagan** received the greatest number of electoral votes when he won with 525. Loser Walter Mondale won only thirteen electoral votes (ten from his home state of Minnesota and three from the District of Columbia). Reagan's electoral victories over **Jimmy Carter** and Walter Mondale totaled 1014–62.

18 WHICH PRESIDENT PARDONED THE GREATEST NUMBER OF PEOPLE?

On May 29, 1865, **Andrew Johnson** granted a pardon to all former confederates who promised to support the Union and obey the laws against slavery.

19 WHICH PRESIDENT SERVED THE SHORTEST FULL SINGLE TERM?

From **John Adams** to **George H. W. Bush,** eleven presidents have served a full single term. Ten of them served for 1,461 days, but **John Adams** served for

Gerald Ford at the University of Michigan

only 1,460 because during his span there was no leap year.

20 WHO WAS OUR MOST ATHLETIC PRESIDENT?

This is, of course, a matter of opinion, but I nominate **Gerald Ford,** who was a star center on the University of Michigan football team. In his *Saturday Night Live* skits, comedian Chevy Chase created an image of Ford as a bumbling stumbler. But consider the facts: Ford turned down offers to play professionally for the Detroit Lions and the Green Bay Packers, opting for the study of law instead. He was head boxing coach and assistant football coach at Yale University. He was an adept tennis player and scored a hole in one in the Memphis Golf Classic.

PATTERNS OF THE
PRESIDENCY

★ ★ ★ ★

WHAT TWO PRESIDENTS DIED ON THE VERY SAME DAY?

Our second and third presidents, **John Adams** and **Thomas Jefferson,** political rivals, then friends, both died on July 4, 1826, exactly fifty years after the adoption of the Declaration of Independence.

As Jefferson lay weak and dying in his home in Monticello on the evening of July 3, he whispered, "Is this the Fourth?" To quiet the former president, his young law-yer-confidante and grandson-in-law, Nicholas Trist, answered, "Yes." Jefferson fell asleep with a smile. His heart continued to beat until the bells and fireworks of the Fourth rang out and exploded the next day.

At dawn of that same day, Adams was expiring in his home in Quincy, Massachusetts. A servant asked the fading Adams, "Do you know what day it is?" "Oh yes," responded the lion in winter. "It is the glorious Fourth of July." He then lapsed into a stupor but awakened in the afternoon to see and hear the celebratory fireworks exploding in the sky. "Thomas Jefferson survives," Adams sighed feebly. He ceased to breathe around sunset, about six hours after Jefferson.

James Monroe also died on July 4, five years later, and **Calvin Coolidge** was born on July 4, 1872. **James Madison** was offered drugs so that he might live until July 4 but refused them and expired on June 28, 1836.

Thomas Jefferson, James Madison, and **James Monroe**—our third, fourth, and fifth presidents—each were elected to two terms as president of the United States. A string of three consecutive presidents, each being elected twice, has happened only one other time in American history. Who were those three presidents?

The answer is **Bill Clinton, George W. Bush,** and **Barack Obama,** our forty-second, forty-third, and forty-fourth chief executives. Almost two centuries elapsed between the two sequences of three presidents filling the space of twenty-four years.

The more we delve into the lives of our American presidents, the more we see patterns that connect their feats, their fates, and their families:

★ For well more than a century, with but a single exception, the party in presidential power has held the Oval Office for multiple terms: 1897–1913: **William McKinley** through **William Howard Taft**—four terms of Republicans; 1913–1921: **Woodrow Wilson**—two terms of a Democrat; 1921–1933: **Warren Harding** through **Herbert Hoover**—three terms of Republicans; 1933–1953: **Franklin Roosevelt** through **Harry Truman**—

five terms of Democrats; 1953–1961: **Dwight Eisenhower**—two terms of a Republican; 1961–1969: **John F. Kennedy** and **Lyndon Johnson**—two terms of Democrats; 1969–1977: **Richard Nixon** and **Gerald Ford**—two terms of Republicans; 1977–1981: **Jimmy Carter**—one term of a Democrat (the only exception to the multiple-term rule); 1981–1993: **Ronald Reagan** and **George H. W. Bush**—three terms of Republicans; 1993–2001: **Bill Clinton**—two terms of a Democrat; 2001–2009: **George W. Bush**—two terms of a Republican; 2009–2017: **Barack Obama**—two terms of a Democrat.

★ Through **George W. Bush,** the ancestry of our first forty-three presidents has been limited to the following seven heritages, or some combination thereof—Dutch, English, German, Irish, Scottish, Swiss, and Welsh. **Barack Obama** was our first president of African heritage, the son of a Kenyan father.

★ The most common religious affiliation has been Episcopalian (twelve); the second most common Presbyterian (eight). Four of our presidents—**Thomas Jefferson, Abraham Lincoln, Andrew Johnson,** and **Rutherford B. Hayes**—had no declared religion. Could they have been elected today?

★ **George Washington** was born in 1732 and **Barack Obama** in 1961. From Washington through Obama, presidents have been born in all the possible decades except for the 1810s, the 1930s, and the 1950s.

★ More than half our presidents (twenty-two) have served as governors, the first being **Thomas Jefferson** (Virginia) and the most recent **George W. Bush** (Texas).

★ More than a third of our presidents (sixteen) have been U.S. senators, the first being **James Monroe** (Virginia) and the most recent **Barack Obama** (Illinois).

★ More than half of our presidents (twenty-three) have been lawyers, the first being **John Adams** and the most recent **Barack Obama.**

★ No American president has grown up as an only child. All have had at least one full sibling, except for **Franklin Roosevelt, Gerald Ford, Bill Clinton,** and **Barack Obama,** who had half siblings. Twelve of our presidents have been firstborn males, while six have been the youngest child in their family.

★ Our forty-four presidents have been the proud fathers of 158 children— ninety-two boys and sixty-five girls. Six of the forty-four men who served as president had no children, the last one being **Warren Harding,** who married a divorcée five years his senior in 1891. The marriage lasted thirty-two years but produced no offspring. The other childless presidents: **James Buchanan, James Polk, Andrew Jackson, James Madison,** and **George Washington.** That Washington was childless helped

Chester Arthur

ensure that the presidency would not become a blood-heir monarchy.

★ **Barack Obama** is only our sixth brown-eyed president. **John Quincy Adams, Andrew Johnson,** and **Chester Arthur** in the nineteenth century, and **Lyndon Johnson** and **Richard Nixon** in the twentieth century were our only other presidents with brown peepers. A surprising thirty-eight of our forty-four presidents have had blue, hazel, or gray eyes.

Harvard University

★ Virginia is the birth state of the greatest number of our presidents, including seven of the first twelve—**George Washington, Thomas Jefferson, James Madison, James Monroe, William Henry Harrison, John Tyler,** and **Zachary Taylor,** as well as **Woodrow Wilson.** Jefferson, Monroe, and Tyler were governors of Virginia.

★ Ohio is known as the "Mother of Presidents" because eight American presidents came from Ohio—**William Henry Harrison, Ulysses S. Grant, Rutherford B. Hayes, James Garfield** (that's three in a row), **Benjamin Harrison, William McKinley, William Howard Taft,** and **Warren Harding.**

★ Harvard University boasts the most presidents as alumni (eight in all)— **John Adams, John Quincy Adams, Rutherford B. Hayes** (law school), **Theodore Roosevelt, Franklin Roosevelt, John Kennedy, George W. Bush** (business school), and **Barack Obama** (law school). Yale University

Barack Obama

is second, with five presidents as alumni—**William Howard Taft, Gerald Ford** (law school), **George H. W. Bush, Bill Clinton,** and **George W. Bush.**

★ Presidents' Day is the official designation of a federal holiday that is now celebrated on the third Monday of February. The original celebration was in honor of **George Washington,** whose actual birthday was February 22. **Abraham Lincoln,** who was born February 12, was added to the mix, and in the late 1980s, Presidents' Day (note the apostrophe after the *s* to indicate that more than one president is being celebrated) became the official name of the holiday. Our American presidents have influenced other holidays:

- **Rutherford B. Hayes** and his wife, Lucy, conducted the first Easter egg roll on the White House lawn.

- In 1916, **Woodrow Wilson** issued a proclamation calling for a nationwide observance of Flag Day on June 14. It was not until 1949 that Congress made this day a permanent observance by resolving that "the fourteenth day of June of each year is hereby designated as Flag Day." The measure was signed into law by **Harry Truman.**

- On November 26, 1789, **George Washington** established the first national celebration of Thanksgiving. In 1863, **Abraham Lincoln,** hoping to unite a sundered nation, issued a proclamation

White House Easter egg roll, 1929

declaring Thanksgiving to be a national holiday to be celebrated on the last Thursday of November. He did this at the urging of Sarah Josepha Hale, the poet and editor who wrote the children's rhyme "Mary Had a Little Lamb." **Franklin Roosevelt** moved Turkey Day up a week to the third Thursday in November—to give Americans more time for Christmas shopping. Controversy followed, and Congress passed a joint resolution in 1941 decreeing that Thanksgiving should fall on the fourth Thursday of each November, where it remains. **John F. Kennedy** established the tradition of granting a presidential pardon to a Thanksgiving turkey, who is then retired—alive and gobbling—to a petting farm.

- The placing of a decorated Christmas tree in the White House began in 1889 on Christmas morning during the presidency of **Benjamin Harrison.** In 1913, **Woodrow Wilson** asked for a community Christmas tree to be placed at the Capitol so that a tree-lighting ceremony could be recognized as a national event.

★ Can you name two presidents, each of whom succeeded his successor? **Grover Cleveland** comes to mind because he was succeeded by Benjamin Harrison, whom he in turn succeeded. The second part of the answer is . . . **Benjamin Harrison.** Here's why: Harrison succeeded Cleveland, who then succeeded Harrison. Thus, Benjamin Harrison also succeeded his successor.

★ Four pairs of presidents defeated each other in successive elections: **John Adams** won out over **Thomas Jefferson** in 1796; Jefferson defeated Adams in 1800. **John Quincy Adams** was selected over **Andrew Jackson** in 1824; Jackson beat out Adams in 1828. **Martin Van Buren** defeated **William Henry Harrison** in 1836; Harrison outpolled Van Buren in 1840.

John Adams

John Quincy Adams

Benjamin Harrison edged **Grover Cleveland** in 1888. Cleveland defeated Harrison in 1892.

★ **John Adams** and **John Quincy Adams** are the only two presidents among our first seven to leave office after a single term.

★ In a form called the double dactyl, John Hollander has written this little ditty about our twenty-third president:

Higgledy-piggledy,
Benjamin Harrison,
Twenty-third president,
Was, and, as such,

Served between Clevelands and
Save for this trivial
Idiosyncrasy,
Didn't do much.

★ Five presidents won the presidency but lost the popular vote: **Andrew Jackson** won the popular vote but lost the election to **John Quincy Adams** (1824); Samuel J. Tilden won the popular vote but lost the election to **Rutherford B. Hayes** (1876); **Grover Cleveland** won the popular vote but lost the election to **Benjamin Harrison** (1888); Al Gore won the popular vote but lost the election to **George W. Bush** (2000); and Hillary Clinton won the popular vote but lost the election to **Donald Trump** (2016).

★ Only thirteen (less than a third) of our forty-four presidents have served at least two terms, including five of the first seven who occupied the office and three of the last four.

★ How about the peculiar presidential parallels between **John Adams** and **George H. W. Bush**? Both were born in Massachusetts and attended Ivy League colleges—Harvard for Adams, Yale for Bush. They both served as ambassadors and were elected as vice president for two terms, serving under popular, older presidents—**George Washington** and **Ronald Reagan.**

Adams and Bush are the only presidents elected immediately after two terms as vice president, and both were president for a single term. Both were defeated for a second term by younger southerners (**Thomas Jefferson** and **Bill Clinton**). Adams and Bush were our only two presidents whose sons also served as presidents. Their sons shared their first names, were also Ivy League graduates, lost the popular vote but not the electoral contest, and succeeded two-term southern presidents (**James Monroe** and **Bill Clinton**).

★ Between **Andrew Jackson** and **Abraham Lincoln,** eight successive presidents served a single term or less—**Martin Van Buren** (1837–1841), **William Henry Harrison** (1841), **John Tyler** (1841–1845), **James Polk** (1845–1849), **Zachary Taylor** (1849–1850), **Millard Fillmore** (1850–1853), **Franklin Pierce** (1853–1857), and **James Buchanan** (1857–1861).

★ Two of our chief executives apparently forgot that they were presidents:

- **Thomas Jefferson** left specific instructions for the message to be carved on his tombstone:

Here was buried Thomas Jefferson

Author of the Declaration of American Independence

of the Statute of Virginia for religious freedom

and Father of the University of Virginia

Do you see what's missing? Apparently Jefferson didn't think it important enough to include his two terms as president of the United States.

- **William Howard Taft**'s lifelong ambition was to be chief justice of the Supreme Court, and he was appointed to that position by **Warren Harding** eight years after his presidency. So rewarding was this turn of events that he later said, "I don't remember that I was ever president."

Thomas Jefferson's grave at Monticello

★ **John Quincy Adams** named his eldest son George Washington.

★ **Martin Van Buren** was the eighth president and the eighth vice president. He lived to see the election of eight different presidents from eight different states.

★ Seven presidents elected at intervals of twenty years died in office—**William**

Tecumseh

Henry Harrison (elected in 1840), **Abraham Lincoln** (1860), **James Garfield** (1880), **William McKinley** (1900), **Warren Harding** (1920), **Franklin Roosevelt** (1940), and **John F. Kennedy** (1960). First noted in a Ripley's Believe It or Not! book published in 1934, this string of untimely presidential deaths is variously known as the curse of Tippecanoe,

the zero-year curse, the twenty-year curse, and Tecumseh's curse, Tecumseh being the chief of the Shawnee Nation defeated by **William Henry Harrison** at the Battle of Tippecanoe in 1811. **Ronald Reagan,** elected in 1980 and shot by John Hinckley Jr. on March 30, 1981, almost continued the deadly sequence but survived and broke the curse.

★ The challenges to the health of our presidents could be collected into an encyclopedia of medical maladies and mishaps. Here are a few of the most famous and bizarre:

- **George Washington** suffered severe tooth loss that made it difficult for him to eat and even speak. He began developing severe dental problems from cracking walnuts with his teeth. At his inauguration, Washington had but a single tooth. At various times he wore dentures made of human teeth, hippopotamus ivory, or lead—never wood. Wooden teeth would have filled Washington's maw full of rotting pulp. Washington's lack of choppers altered the shape of his once-handsome face, resulting in the famous pinched look in his later portraits. Because Martha Washington had delivered four children during her previous marriage, it appears that Washington's infertility was the reason that the Father of Our Country never became a father.

- A contemporary reporter for the *New York Herald* described **Abraham Lincoln** thusly: "a tall, lank, lean man considerably over six feet in height with long, pendulous arms terminating in hands of extraordinary dimension which, however, were far exceeded in proportion by his feet." Lincoln's physical dimensions have led many a medical detective to conjecture that he was a victim of Marfan syndrome, a connective tissue disorder.

- **Ulysses S. Grant** claimed to smoke seven to ten cigars a day. When

word got out of Grant's love of stogies, people sent him more than ten thousand boxes of cigars. He died of throat cancer. For the last few months of his life he had to sleep in an easy chair to avoid choking.

John L. Sullivan

- In 1893, at the start of his second term, **Grover Cleveland** was diagnosed with cancer and secretly underwent an operation to have a portion of his left jaw replaced with a rubber substitute. The surgery was conducted on the presidential yacht and was not disclosed to the press or even the vice president until after Cleveland's presidency. That's because the country was going through a financial crisis that might have been made more severe by news that the president's life was in danger.

- At Harvard, **Theodore Roosevelt** almost won the lightweight boxing championship. While boxing in the White House with heavyweight champion John L. Sullivan, Roosevelt received a blow to his face that left him blind in his left eye. He was so nearsighted in the other eye that he always carried a dozen pairs of glasses with him in case he needed a replacement.

- Perhaps because of chronic depression, **Calvin Coolidge** slept eleven hours a day and always took an afternoon nap lasting at least two hours. Social observer H. L. Mencken wrote of Coolidge, "His chief feat during five years and seven months in office was to sleep more than any other President—to sleep more and say less." At a performance of the Marx Brothers show *Animal Crackers,* Groucho Marx discovered Coolidge in the audience and cried out to him, "Isn't it past your bedtime, Cal?" The president laughed heartily, along with the audience. When *New Yorker* writer and wit Dorothy Parker was informed that Calvin Coolidge had died, she asked, "How can they tell?"

- At the age of thirty-nine, **Franklin Roosevelt** was paralyzed by polio. He served his entire presidency without the use of his legs, but through rigorous exercise, learned to stand with the help of braces. His wheelchair was designed with no arms to give the appearance of a regular chair. Roosevelt seldom mentioned his polio but once observed, "If you had spent two years in bed trying to wiggle your big toe, after that anything else would seem easy."

- **John F. Kennedy** may well have been the worst medical mess ever to occupy the White House. His maladies—colitis, steroid complications, chronic back pain, and Addison's disease, with resulting chronic fatigue, to name just a few—were kept from the public eye before Kennedy's election and during his service as president.

Franklin Roosevelt with Ruthie Bie and Fala, 1941

★ Thirty-one of our forty-four presidents have served in the military. (All presidents have been commander in chief, but that does not strictly count as military service.)

★ **John Tyler** was born when **George Washington** was president. His youngest daughter, Mary, born when Tyler was seventy years of age, died during the administration of **Harry Truman.** That's a span of thirty-two presidents—more than 150 years. As of the writing of this book, Harrison Tyler, a grandson (I didn't say "great-grandson") of John Tyler, is still alive.

★ From **Abraham Lincoln** through **Benjamin Harrison,** every president to have a beard has been a Republican.

★ **George Washington** (in his younger days), **Franklin Pierce, Warren Harding, John F. Kennedy, Gerald Ford** (in his younger days), and **Ronald Reagan** are generally ranked as our handsomest presidents. At least two other presidents have been able to joke about their unbecoming looks:

• The *New York Herald* described **Abraham Lincoln** thusly: "Lincoln is the leanest, lankiest, most ungainly mass of legs, arms, and hatchet-face ever strung upon a single frame. He has most unwarrantably abused the privilege which all politicians have of being ugly." Lincoln was known to make fun of his legendary homeliness and gangly height. During one of their debates, Stephen Douglas accused Lincoln

Ronald Reagan as radio announcer, 1930s

of being two faced. Replied Lincoln calmly, "I leave it to my audience: If I had two faces, would I be wearing this one?" When a grouchy old Democrat said to him, "They say you are a self-made man," Lincoln riposted, "Well, all I've got to say is that it was a damned bad job." Lincoln was frequently compared to a monkey, an ape, and an "ape baboon," if such a thing is possible. One wonders if that had anything to do with the happenstance that Lincoln and Charles Darwin were both born on February 12, 1809.

- **Woodrow Wilson** composed a limerick to poke fun at his horsy visage:

For beauty I am not a star.
There are others more handsome
by far.
But my face, I don't mind it
Because I'm behind it.
It's the people in front whom I jar.

★ **James Garfield** entertained friends by writing Latin with one hand and Greek with the other. He was primarily left-handed, along with presidents **Harry Truman, Gerald Ford, George H. W. Bush, Bill Clinton,** and **Barack Obama.** Four of the past eight presidents have been southpaws.

★ Three U.S. presidents have been the sons of clergymen—**Chester Arthur, Grover Cleveland,** and **Woodrow Wilson.**

★ **William McKinley** was the last president to have fought in the Civil War. **Ulysses S. Grant, Rutherford B. Hayes** (the only one who was wounded), **James Garfield, Chester Arthur,** and **Benjamin Harrison** were the others. McKinley had been an aide-de-camp to another future president, General Rutherford B. Hayes.

★ Both **Theodore Roosevelt** and **Franklin Roosevelt** served as governor of New York and as assistant secretary of the navy.

Grace Coolidge with pet raccoon Rebecca

★ During their terms of service, all but two of our presidents—**Millard Fillmore** and **Chester Arthur**—had pets. Two of our chief executives were stunningly imaginative (dare we say compulsive?) animal collectors:

- **Theodore Roosevelt,** at various times in his presidency, owned six dogs, two cats, a gray squirrel, a pony, a pig, a badger, a garter snake, a piebald rat, four guinea pigs, a hen, a macaw, and a one-legged rooster.

- **Calvin Coolidge,** at various times in his presidency, owned six dogs, a cat (which would cleave to his clothing as he walked around the White House), two raccoons, a donkey, a goose, a bobcat, a wallaby, two lion cubs, an antelope, and a pygmy hippo!

★ Two other twentieth-century presidents kept farm animals outside the White House:

- **William Howard Taft** kept a cow on the White House lawn to supply him with fresh milk. He was the last president to do so.

- During **Woodrow Wilson**'s presidency, his wife introduced a flock of sheep to graze on the White House lawn. Their wool was sold to raise money for the Red Cross during World War I. One newspaper inadvertently left out the word sheep when it wrote, "Woodrow Wilson's wife grazed on the front lawn of the White House."

★ At least two of our presidents have had something to say about the art and science of spelling:

- **Andrew Jackson,** whom some accused of being illiterate, observed, "It's a damn small mind that can think of only one way to spell a word."

One of the original teddy bears, owned by Theodore Roosevelt's grandson, Kermit

- **Theodore Roosevelt** was an enthusiastic champion of simplified spelling. In 1906, he sent his annual message to Congress in simplified spelling. "Nuthing escapes Mr. Rucevelt," wrote the *Louisville Courier-Journal.* "No subject is tu hi fr him to takl, nor tu lo for him tu notis."

★ **Theodore Roosevelt** and **Ronald Reagan** were each responsible for the success of two major commercial products:

- Early in 1903, a stuffed animal then known as "teddy's bear" began to gain what would become enormous and enduring popularity. The manufacturers, Rose and Morris Michtom, who ran a novelty store in Brooklyn, claimed that they received permission from President **Theodore Roosevelt** to create and distribute the toy. Roosevelt used the bear as a symbol in his successful 1904 presidential election. Now, more than a century later, children still hug their adorable teddy bears.

- **Theodore Roosevelt** was prone to asthma attacks as a child, and on doctor's orders, began drinking coffee to arrest these onslaughts. Over time, he grew to love coffee. In 1907, the president took a drink of coffee at an exhibition booth, and when offered a second cup he exclaimed, "Delighted! It's good to the last drop!" Maxwell House brand coffee took their motto from that exclamation, and it remains theirs even to this day, more than a century later.

- **Ronald Reagan** generated booming sales of two products—hearing aids, because he used one, and jelly beans, because he told reporters he liked them.

★ **George Washington, John Adams,** and **Thomas Jefferson** were all avid collectors and players of marbles. **John Tyler** was playing marbles when he learned that he had become president. But golf is the sport most associated with American presidents:

- Seventeen of our most recent twenty presidents have played golf.

- **William Howard Taft** was the first president to take up the game.

- **Woodrow Wilson** was adamant about playing golf year-round and any time of day. He used red balls for snow days and had his caddie

William Howard Taft on the links

tote a large flashlight for play at night. One particular match didn't end until five o'clock in the morning. Wilson claimed that golf was a game of amusement, not competition, and seldom kept score. On several occasions his wife, Edith, joined him on the links, a rarity for a woman, let alone a First Lady.

- The most notable golfer among presidents, **Dwight Eisenhower** played golf as many as 150 days a year, and often walked the halls of the White House with a pitching wedge. Eisenhower had a putting green installed on the White House lawn and a driving range in the basement. Located at the seventeenth hole at Augusta National Golf Club is a loblolly pine officially called the "Eisenhower Tree." The former president and club member hit into the tree so often he campaigned to have it cut down, a proposal rejected by the club's board of governors. The pine has been linked to Eisenhower ever since. When

Ike ran for reelection in 1956, there were bumper stickers that quipped, "Ben Hogan for president. If we're going to have a golfer—let's have a good one!" In 2009, Eisenhower was posthumously elected to the World Golf Hall of Fame.

- Despite a bad back and lack of practice, **John F. Kennedy** often shot in the mid- to high seventies.

- **Richard Nixon** scored a hole in one on Labor Day, 1961, at the Bel-Air Country Club in Los Angeles. **Dwight Eisenhower** aced the par-three thirteenth hole at Seven Lakes Country Club in Palm Springs.

- **Gerald Ford** hit many a stellar golf shot in pro-am tournaments (including the aforementioned hole in one in the Memphis Golf Classic), but he became best known for peppering galleries with wild hooks and topped liners that occasionally met somebody's limb or head. Ford was often paired with comedian Bob Hope, who stoked the president's reputation when he called him "the man who made golf a contact sport" and "the most dangerous driver since Ben-Hur." Hope once zinged, "It's not hard to find Jerry Ford on a golf course—you just follow the wounded." On another occasion Hope quipped, "Whenever I play with him, I usually try to make it a foursome—the president, myself, a paramedic, and a faith healer." He added, "I'm comfortable playing with [Ford] as long as my caddie and I have the same blood type."

Gerald Ford playing golf

- **George H. W. Bush** and **George W. Bush** come from a prominent golfing family that includes H. W.'s grandfather, George Herbert Walker, founder of the Walker Cup tournament, and H. W.'s father Prescott Bush, who served as head of the USGA.

★ **William Howard Taft** and **John F. Kennedy** are the only two presidents to be buried in Arlington National Cemetery.

★ Given the high-stakes gamble of being president, it's no surprise that at least six of our presidents have played the game of poker:

- The first president who we are sure played poker was **Grover Cleveland.** He was an especially hard-working president and took time off on many a Sunday afternoon to play the game. "My father used to say that it was wicked to go fishing on Sunday," he once explained, "but he never said anything about draw poker."

- **Warren Harding**'s advisers were known as the Poker Cabinet because they frequently played poker together. Harding played at least twice a week, while liquor flowed freely despite Prohibition. Once Harding gambled away a priceless set of White House china dating back to the administration of **Rutherford B. Hayes.**

- Because of paraplegia brought on by his polio, **Franklin Roosevelt** was unable to relax by taking long walks or playing golf or tennis. But he often had dinner with his poker-playing pals and then adjourned to a marathon session of cards. His favorite game was seven-card stud. Among the regulars were the vice president, Speaker of the House, attorney general, secretary of commerce, and at least one Supreme Court justice. The president's secretary, "Missy" LeHand, served

*Warren Harding with a good
night's poker winnings*

cocktails and often played in the game. One of the rules was that nobody could discuss anything serious at the evening poker sessions. The only thought was how to outfox the other players.

- Roosevelt selected as his last vice president another poker player. **Harry Truman** was playing poker when he found out that he had become president. Truman was known as an excellent poker player, and "The buck stops here" became the famous slogan of his administration. (The "buck" actually refers to a betting marker in poker.) In office for just a few months, Truman had to decide whether or not to drop the atomic bomb on Japanese cities in order to bring World War II to a close. To help him focus during the decision-making process, Truman engaged in an almost continuous game of pot-limit poker aboard the presidential yacht, the *Williamsburg*. Often all three branches of government were represented at the poker table. The group would board the ship Friday afternoon and sail the Potomac until Sunday afternoon.

- Born a Quaker, **Richard Nixon** remained unfamiliar with any form of gambling until his mid-twenties. But during his World War II years in the Navy, Nixon won $6,000, which helped to fund his initial—and successful—run for Congress.

- **Barack Obama** was our first poker-playing president in thirty-six years.

★ **Theodore Roosevelt** gave away his niece Eleanor Roosevelt at her wedding to **Franklin Roosevelt.** Franklin Roosevelt was a fifth cousin of Theodore Roosevelt, a fifth cousin once removed of his wife, Eleanor Roosevelt, and a seventh cousin once removed of Winston Churchill. Genealogists have determined that FDR was related to eleven other presidents: **George Washington, John Adams, James Madison, John Quincy Adams, Martin Van Buren, William Henry Harrison, Zachary Taylor, Ulysses S. Grant, Benjamin Harrison, Theodore Roosevelt,** and **William Howard Taft.**

★ A temperance committee visited **Abraham Lincoln** and asked him to fire General **Ulysses S. Grant.** Surprised, Lincoln asked why. "He drinks too much," answered the spokesman for the group. "Well," said Lincoln, "I wish some of you would tell me the brand of whiskey that Grant drinks. I would like to send a barrel of it to every one of my other generals."

★ Kentucky contributed a president to each side of the Civil War—**Abraham Lincoln** and Jefferson Davis.

Jimmy Carter

★ Because of the Watergate scandals, many accuse **Richard Nixon** of having been the most nefarious president in our history. Not so in 1960, the year in which Nixon lost an extremely close presidential election to **John F. Kennedy.** Accusations of voting fraud flew, and Nixon was encouraged to protest the result. But he stepped aside, explaining, "If I were to demand a recount, the organization of the new administration and the orderly transfer of responsibility from the old to the new might be delayed for months. The situation within the entire federal government would be chaotic." Years later, Nixon's successor, **Gerald Ford,** would use the same logic when he pardoned Nixon of all crimes.

★ In 1965, **Lyndon Johnson** issued the first Medicare card. The recipient was **Harry Truman.**

★ One of our most intelligent presidents, **Jimmy Carter** could speed-read two thousand words per minute. Carter and **Herbert Hoover** were our only two presidents who were engineers. **John F. Kennedy** constantly astounded all those around him with his knowledge of current events. It is said that he could read four newspapers in twenty minutes.

★ **George H. W. Bush** was the first president born in June. Before Bush, presidents had been born during the other eleven months.

★ As a delegate to Boys Nation while in high school, **Bill Clinton** met President **John F. Kennedy** in the White House Rose Garden in 1962. The encounter led him to enter a life of public service. Years earlier, **Franklin Roosevelt**'s parents visited their friend, President **Grover Cleveland,** in the White House. Cleveland looked little five-year-old Franklin in the eye and wearily declared, "My little man, I am making a strange wish for you, a wish I suppose no one else could make. It is my wish you never be the president of the United States." Roosevelt grew

up to become the only president who served four terms.

★ Formerly bitter political rivals **George H. W. Bush** and **Bill Clinton** joined forces to raise funds for victims of the Indian Ocean tsunami in 2004 and Hurricane Katrina in 2005.

★ **Bill Clinton,** our forty-second president, nominated **Barack Obama,** our forty-fourth president, as a candidate for reelection. That connection is unique.

★ **George Washington**'s salary as president was $25,000, **Barack Obama**'s $400,000. But Washington's would be worth about $531,000 today.

★ The election of 2016, pitting **Donald Trump** and Mike Pence against Hillary Clinton and Tim Kaine, included no incumbent running for office. Similarly, in the election of 2008, neither incumbent president **George W. Bush** nor vice president Dick Cheney ran for office. The last time before that we had a presidential election in which no incumbent ran was 1952, when **Dwight Eisenhower** and Richard Nixon defeated Adlai Stevenson and John Sparkman. 1952 was also the last year that a nomination went more than one round in a convention, in this case the Democratic convention.

★ Despite an inclination for presidents to bloviate, at least two of our chief executives have praised the value of speaking briefly and to the point:

- Once a cabinet member praised **Woodrow Wilson** for his short speeches and asked him how long it took him to prepare them. "It depends," Wilson told him. "If I am to speak ten minutes, I need a week for preparation; if fifteen minutes, three days; if half an hour, two days; if an hour, I am ready now."

- **Franklin Roosevelt,** one of the finest orators to be president, had this advice about the art of public speaking: "Be sincere; be brief; be seated."

Woodrow Wilson

PRESIDENTS
UNDER FIRE

THE ORIGINAL ASSASSINS were a militant branch of Shiite Muslims who opposed the rule of Sunni caliphs from the eighth to the fourteenth centuries. The word *Assassin* was derived from *hashshashin*, "hashish user," because it was thought that these militants ingested hashish to inspire them to commit political murder.

★ Four presidents have died from assassins' bullets—**Abraham Lincoln** in 1865, **James Garfield** in 1881, **William McKinley** in 1901, and **John F. Kennedy** in 1963:

★ When the Civil War ended, **Abraham Lincoln,** on April 13, 1865, gave orders to stop the draft of soldiers. The following day he made his fatal visit to Ford's Theatre to see *Our American Cousin.* At one point in the play the heroine, reclining on a garden seat, calls for a shawl to protect her from the draft. The actor Edward Southern, to whom the request was addressed, replied on this occasion with this impromptu line: "You are mistaken, Miss Mary. The draft has already been stopped by order of the president!" Lincoln joined in the audience appreciation of this remark with what was to be his last laugh. On that fatal night, Lincoln did not want to go to the theater. He had seen *Our American Cousin* once before and was not eager to see it again. But Mary Todd Lincoln had promised his presence, so he attended.

★ In the weeks following **Abraham Lincoln**'s assassination, many people paid their respects at the White House—and made off with thousands of dollars of looted objects.

★ Robert Todd Lincoln, Abraham's eldest son, arrived too late to stop three separate presidential assassinations. He saw his father at Ford's Theatre, but only after John Wilkes Booth had fired the fatal shot. By invitation, he went to a Washington train station in 1881

John Wilkes Booth

to meet **James Garfield,** arriving only minutes after Garfield was shot. Again by invitation, he traveled to Buffalo, New York, in 1901 to meet **William McKinley,** but got there after the fatal shot had already been fired. Robert Todd Lincoln lived for a quarter century after the death of McKinley, but made it known that he wanted no further invitations from any president of the United States.

★ After **James Garfield** was shot by Charles Guiteau, he spent eighty days on his deathbed while a team of doctors probed him with unwashed hands and unsanitary medical instruments. They tried to find the bullet with a metal detector invented by Alexander Graham Bell—but the device failed because Garfield was placed on a bed with metal springs, which the metal detector mistakenly identified as the bullet. To escape the Washington heat, Garfield was moved to a seaside cottage in New Jersey early in September 1881. There he died on September 19, succumbing to death by doctors. At

Guiteau's trial, the assassin admitted to shooting Garfield but claimed that it was the doctors who killed the president. Guiteau was hanged anyway.

★ **William McKinley** became the third president to be assassinated in office. The assassin was an anarchist, Leon Czolgosz, who shot the president in 1901 at the Pan-American Exposition

William McKinley

in Buffalo. Virtually the first words out of the president's mouth were to his secretary, George Cortelyou: "My wife—be careful, Cortelyou, how you tell her. Oh, be careful!" When he saw his assassin being beaten to the ground, he cried out, "Don't let them hurt him!"

★ Tragically, a back brace that **John F. Kennedy** wore on the day of his assassination actually held him in place as a second and third shot fired by Lee Harvey Oswald riddled his body.

★ Ever since the assassination of **John F. Kennedy** on November 22, 1963, historians have pointed out a number of striking similarities between Kennedy's life and death and those of **Abraham Lincoln.** You be the judge as to whether these convergences are significant or mere coincidences:

- Lincoln was elected to the House of Representatives in 1846, Kennedy in 1946. Lincoln failed to win the vice presidential nomination in 1856, Kennedy in 1956. Lincoln was elected to the presidency in 1860, Kennedy in 1960. Lincoln defeated Stephen Douglas, born in 1813; Kennedy defeated Richard Nixon, born in 1913. Neither victor received 50 percent of the popular vote. Both presidents lost sons during their presidencies: Willie Lincoln succumbed to typhoid fever, and Patrick Kennedy was stillborn.

- The last names of both presidents are each composed of seven letters. Both presidents had vice presidents named Johnson, both older than their presidents. The names of both vice presidents total an unlucky thirteen letters. **Andrew Johnson** was born in 1808, **Lyndon Johnson** in 1908. Andrew Johnson served in the House of Representatives in 1847, Lyndon Johnson in 1947.

- Lincoln and Kennedy repeatedly spoke of having vivid dreams of assassination attempts. (In a dream, Lincoln heard weeping and wailing over the death of the president. He entered a room and viewed a coffin that contained his own body.) Each was warned by advisers not to attend the fatal event. Both assassins—John Wilkes Booth and Lee Harvey Oswald—were known by three names totaling fifteen letters.

- Lincoln was assassinated in Ford's Theatre, Kennedy in a Ford automobile—a Lincoln. Each was shot on a Friday in the back of the head, each with his wife nearby. Booth shot Lincoln in a theater and was captured in a barn; Oswald shot Kennedy from a warehouse and was arrested at a theater. Neither assassin lived to stand trial.

★ Six presidents were luckier and survived assassination attempts—**Andrew Jackson, Theodore Roosevelt, Franklin Roosevelt, Harry Truman, Gerald Ford,** and **Ronald Reagan.**

- **Andrew Jackson** was the target of the first attempted assassination of an American president. On January 30, 1835, a mentally disturbed unemployed house painter named Richard Lawrence fired two different guns at the president from point-blank range. When both weapons failed to fire, Jackson then chased after Lawrence and beat him with his cane. The odds of two consecutive misfires were estimated at 125,000 to 1.

- The only former president to be the target of an attempted assassination, **Theodore Roosevelt** was shot on October 14, 1912, just before giving a speech in Milwaukee during his run as Bull Moose candidate. Even though the bullet lodged four inches deep in his chest, he still delivered the speech. "I don't know whether you fully understand that I have been shot," he told the stunned audience, "but it takes more than that to kill a Bull Moose." He was saved from certain death by the metal glasses case and the speech text that he had placed in his breast pocket.

- **Gerald Ford** is the only president to have been shot at by a woman. Lynette "Squeaky" Fromme, a former member of the Charles Manson "family," aimed a pistol at the president but did not get off a shot. Just seventeen days later, Sara Jane Moore fired a bullet at Ford. The bullet struck a nearby taxi driver.

- When **Ronald Reagan** was shot by would-be assassin John Hinckley Jr., in 1981, he quipped, "I forgot to duck." A few hours after surgery, he quoted Winston Churchill: "There is no more exhilarating feeling than being shot at without result." Two hours later, he laughed, "If I had had this much attention in Hollywood, I'd have stayed there." Reagan is the only sitting president to have been wounded by an assassin's bullet and to have survived.

★ **Theodore Roosevelt, John F. Kennedy,** and **Ronald Reagan** were all members of the National Rifle Association—and they were all shot.

Whiskey Rebellion

★ To be president is to suffer the slings and arrows of outraged citizens, but several of our presidents have found themselves under fire—and not just by assassins:

- During the Whiskey Rebellion, in 1794, **George Washington** took personal command of the troops to suppress the rebellion. He was fired on by angry rebels.

- During the War of 1812, when the British marched on Washington,

James Madison was among those who went out to Bladensburg, Maryland, to view the battle. Under fire, he was forced to flee when the American army broke.

- When **Andrew Jackson** was five years old, his mother saw him crying and ordered, "Don't let me see you cry again! Girls were made to cry; boys were made to fight!"

Andrew Jackson

Jackson is said to have fought in more than a hundred duels. A bullet from one of those duels remained lodged close to Jackson's heart until the day he died. During the presidential campaign of 1828, the Whigs circulated a thick pamphlet titled *Reminiscences; or an Extract from the Catalogue of General Jackson's Youthful Indiscretions, Between the Age of Twenty-Three and Sixty.* The diatribe listed fourteen fights, duels, brawls, and shooting affairs in which Jackson "killed, slashed, and clawed various American citizens."

- In 1844, Captain Robert Stockton (later of Stockton, California, fame) had a steamship made to his order. He also had a pair of cannon, of 12-inch bore, fabricated, one of his own design and called the "Peacemaker." Stockton took a VIP party out for a cruise on the Potomac River to show off his new ship and entertain his guests by firing his immense gun. The list of dignitaries included the recently widowed president, **John Tyler,** members of Tyler's cabinet, military brass, senators, a former senator, David Gardiner, and his two daughters, Julia and Margaret. After a lunch below, when the guests called for another firing of the gun, President Tyler, deeply in conversation with Julia Gardiner, stayed below. The gun blew up, killing five people in the party and wounding many more, including David Gardiner. President Tyler not only comforted Julia Gardiner, he soon married her. Her conversation with him saved his life.

- During the Confederate attack on Fort Stevens, **Abraham Lincoln** journeyed to the front to inspect Union defenses. The task of showing him around fell to young Oliver Wendell Holmes Jr., aide to the commanding general, and a future Supreme Court justice. When Holmes pointed out the enemy in the distance, Lincoln stood up—all 6 feet 4 inches of him and a high stovepipe hat, too—to have a look. A snarl of musket fire darted from the enemy trenches. Grabbing the president by the arm, Holmes dragged him under cover and shouted, "Get down, you fool!" When he realized what he had said and to whom, Holmes was sure that disciplinary action would follow. But to his immense relief, Lincoln rejoined, "Captain Holmes, I'm glad to see you know how to talk to a civilian."

Oliver Wendell Holmes Jr.

★ ★ ★ ★

PRESIDENTS
IN THE MEDIA

IN WARM WEATHER, **John Quincy Adams** customarily went skinny-dipping in the Potomac River. The first American woman to become a professional journalist, Anne Royall, knew of Adams's 5:00 a.m. swims. After being refused interviews with Adams many times, she went to the river, gathered his clothes, and sat on them until she had her interview from the president, who spoke to her while chin deep in the water. Before this, no female had interviewed a president.

William Henry Harrison was the first presidential candidate to campaign actively. His was the first campaign slogan: "Tippecanoe and Tyler Too," which was also part of the first campaign song:

> *What's the cause of this commotion,*
> *motion, motion,*
> *Our country through?*
> *It is the ball a-rolling on*
> *For Tippecanoe and Tyler too.*
> *For Tippecanoe and Tyler too.*

> *And with them we'll beat little Van,*
> *Van, Van,*
> *Van is a used up man.*
> *And with them we'll beat little Van.*

"Ball a-rolling" refers to one group of Whig party members who rolled a ten-foot paper, leather, and tin ball emblazoned with pro-Harrison slogans for hundreds of miles from one campaign rally to another. The song gave us the enduring expression "keep the ball rolling." "Little Van" refers to the sitting president, **Martin Van Buren,** who at 5 feet 6 inches tall was our second-shortest president. The campaign tactics worked: Harrison won in a landslide.

The presidency can be like a good steak—a rare medium well done. Mass media—from portraiture to sculpture, from currency to stamps, from literature to newspapers, from the telephone to radio to television—extend the images and sounds of our chief executives and embed them in our national consciousness.

★ **John Tyler** was the first president to be photographed while serving as president. **John Quincy Adams, Andrew Jackson,** and **Martin Van Buren** were all photographed after serving their terms. Until **Abraham Lincoln,** most Americans had no idea what our first fifteen presidents looked and sounded like. Nowadays, with the colossal outreach of mass media, so many of our hopes, dreams, and ideals are inextricably bound up with the persona of the American president.

★ Portraits of presidents **Abraham Lincoln** (on the penny, and the only one facing right), **Thomas Jefferson** (nickel), **Franklin Roosevelt** (dime), **George Washington** (quarter), and **John F. Kennedy** (half dollar) appear on U.S. coins now in production. In 2007, the U.S. government started issuing one-dollar coins featuring images of the American presidents, four each year and in the order of their service.

★ Portraits of presidents **George Washington** (on the $1 bill), **Thomas Jefferson** ($2), **Abraham Lincoln** ($5), **Andrew Jackson** ($20), and **Ulysses S. Grant** ($50) appear on U.S. paper currency now in production. Other presidents appeared on denominations no longer produced: **William McKinley** ($500), **Grover Cleveland** ($1,000), **James Madison** ($5,000), and **Woodrow Wilson** ($100,000).

★ From left to right, the images of presidents **George Washington, Thomas Jefferson, Theodore Roosevelt,** and **Abraham Lincoln** appear on Mount Rushmore, located in the Black Hills of South Dakota, twenty-three miles southwest of Rapid City.

★ **George Washington**'s profile appears on the Purple Heart.

★ PRESIDENTS IN THE MEDIA ★

★ Thomas Nast, perhaps the most famous political cartoonist in our history, was responsible for the popularity of two party animals. During the election of 1828, opponents of **Andrew Jackson** labeled him a "jackass" for his populist beliefs. Jackson was entertained by the notion and ended up using it to his advantage on his campaign posters. Nast is credited with making the donkey the recognized symbol of the Democratic Party, through one of his cartoons that appeared in *Harper's Weekly* in 1870. Four years later, also in *Harper's Weekly,* Nast drew a donkey clothed in lion's skin scaring away all the animals at the zoo. One of those animals, the elephant, was labeled "The Republican Vote." That's all it took for the elephant to become associated with Republicans.

★ In late 1962, out came a humor record titled *The First Family.* Comedian and impersonator Vaughn Meader represented President **John F. Kennedy** and his Boston accent spot on, and the record sold more than seven million

Thomas Nast's donkey and elephant became symbols of the Democratic and Republican Parties

copies in just a few months. After President Kennedy was assassinated, the producers stopped distribution and destroyed all unused copies.

★ Some presidents have known famous authors:

- Nathaniel Hawthorne, author of such American classics as *The Scarlet Letter,* died on a canoe trip in the White Mountains of New Hampshire, accompanied by **Franklin Pierce.** Hawthorne had been Pierce's classmate at Bowdoin College, along with Henry Wadsworth Longfellow.

- **James Garfield** adored the work of General Lew Wallace, the author of *Ben-Hur.* The president appointed Wallace as an ambassador to Constantinople, hoping that the novelist might be inspired to write another exciting book about biblical times. When Charles Dickens toured the United States, Garfield attended his lectures and enjoyed them thoroughly.

- **Theodore Roosevelt** was without doubt one of our most ebullient presidents. The wildly popular

Rudyard Kipling

British adventure writer Rudyard Kipling spent some time with the president and reported: "I curled up in the seat opposite, and listened and wondered, until the universe seemed to be spinning around, and Theodore was the spinner."

- During the administration of **Dwight Eisenhower,** James

Michener, author of *Hawaii, The Source,* and other megasellers, was invited to a celebrity dinner at the White House. Michener declined to attend and explained: "Dear Mr. President: I received your invitation three days after I had agreed to speak a few words at a dinner honoring the wonderful high school teacher who taught me how to write. I know you will not miss me at your dinner, but she might at hers." Michener received a handwritten reply from the understanding Ike: "In his lifetime a man lives under fifteen or sixteen presidents, but a really fine teacher comes into his life but rarely. Go and speak at your teacher's dinner."

★ Other presidents have themselves attained literary fame:

• Perhaps the most iconic tale of presidential virtue is that of young **George Washington** admitting to his father that he chopped down a cherry tree in the family garden: "I cannot tell a lie, father, you know I cannot tell a lie! I did cut it with my little hatchet." This episode, which lives on in almost every grammar school across our fair land, is in fact almost certainly fiction. The story was made up out of whole cloth by Parson Mason Locke Weems in his biography *A History of the the Life and Death, Virtues and Exploits of General George Washington,* a best seller published immediately after the president's death.

• When the British novelist William Makepeace Thackeray used **George Washington** as a character in *The Virginians,* many Americans were appalled. One critic snapped, "Washington was not like other men, and to bring his character down to the level of the vulgar passions of common life is to give lie to the grandest chapter in the uninspired annals of the human race."

• One of the best known of American poems begins:

Walt Whitman

O Captain! my Captain! our fearful trip is done;
The ship has weathered every rack, the prize we sought is won.

In this poem by Walt Whitman, the captain is **Abraham Lincoln.**

- As a young man, **Abraham Lincoln** read and reread the King James Bible, *Aesop's Fables,* Shakespeare, John Bunyan, Daniel Defoe, and Robert Burns. By the time he became president he had developed a distinguished prose style of his own—simple, clear, precise, forceful, rhythmic, poetic, and at times majestic. **John Adams, Thomas Jefferson, Ulysses S. Grant, Theodore Roosevelt,** and **Woodrow Wilson** all possessed unusual literary skills, but at his best, Lincoln towered above them all. The critic Jacques Barzun called him a "literary genius."

- About **Abraham Lincoln**'s Gettysburg Address, the *Chicago Times* review had this to say: "The cheek of every American must tingle with shame as he reads the silly, flat and dish-watery utterances of the man who has been pointed out to intelligent foreigners as the President of the United States."

- The IRS Form 1040 EZ contains 418 words, and the back of a Lay's potato chips bag 401. In the brief compass of 272 words, President Lincoln transformed a gruesome battle into the raison d'être of a truly *United* States that for the first time in its history became a union. Before Lincoln, people used "the United States" as a plural: "The United States *are* . . . ." Ever after it would be "The United States *is* . . . ." That same day at Gettysburg, November 19, 1863, Edward Everett, famed for his oratory, spoke for close to two hours, while Lincoln took only a couple of minutes. Afterwards, Everett took Lincoln aside and said, "My speech will soon be forgotten; yours never will. How gladly would I exchange my hundred pages for your twenty lines!"

- Even while a sundered nation was slaughtering itself on the battlefields of the Civil War, Lincoln could still find time, on November 21, 1864, to write this letter to Lydia Bixby:

"Dear Madam: I have been shown in the files of the War Department a statement of the Adjutant-General of Massachusetts that you are the mother of five sons who have died gloriously on the field of battle. I feel how weak and fruitless must be any words of mine which should

Edward Everett

attempt to beguile you from the grief of a loss so overwhelming. But I cannot refrain from tendering to you the consolation that may be found in the thanks of the Republic they died to save. I pray that our Heavenly Father may assuage the anguish of your bereavement, and leave you only the cherished memory of the loved and lost, and the solemn pride that must be yours to have laid so costly a sacrifice upon the altar of freedom. Yours very sincerely and respectfully, A. Lincoln."

- **Ulysses S. Grant** finished his 200,000-word *Memoirs* only a few days before his death, so he never saw the work published. The book ultimately brought in $450,000 for his family. It remains one of the finest accounts of the Civil War ever written. Grant's popular autobiography was published by his friend Mark Twain in 1885, the same year that Twain came out with *The Adventures of Huckleberry Finn.*

- **Herbert Hoover** wrote approximately sixteen books, including one called *Fishing for Fun and to Wash Your Soul.*

- **John F. Kennedy** is the only president to receive the Pulitzer Prize— for his book *Profiles in Courage.*

Ulysses S. Grant writing his memoirs

- **Jimmy Carter** is our most writerly president, having written about twenty books, many of which have been best sellers. Carter wrote most of his books after his presidency and some with his wife, Rosalynn, as coauthor. In 2003, Carter published the novel *The Hornet's Nest,* a fictional story of the Revolutionary War in the South. Carter remains the only president to have written a published novel. He also wrote a children's book titled *The Little Baby Snoogle-Fleejer,* illustrated by his daughter, Amy.

Calvin Coolidge

★ **Rutherford B. Hayes** remarked to Alexander Graham Bell, "The telephone is an interesting invention, but who would ever want to use one of them?" Nonetheless, in 1879, Hayes became the first president to use a telephone while in office. **Grover Cleveland** personally answered the White House phone. **Calvin Coolidge** hated telephones and never answered them. **William McKinley** was the first president to campaign by telephone.

★ **Abraham Lincoln** is the president most portrayed in the movies, more than 150 of them, but at least two of our presidents have acted in dramatic films:

- **Grover Cleveland** was our first presidential movie star. In 1895, Cleveland agreed to be filmed signing a bill into law. The movie was called *A Capital Courtship,* and it was a big hit on the lyceum circuit.

Ronald Reagan with first wife Jane Wyman

- **Ronald Reagan** was our only president to have been a professional actor, appearing in fifty-four Hollywood films. That number might have reached fifty-five, but Reagan was refused a part in the film version of *The Best Man* because he "did not look presidential enough." Divorced from movie star Jane Wyman, Reagan and his second wife, Nancy Davis, appeared opposite each other in one film, *Hellcats of the Navy.* Movie star William Holden was the best man at the Reagans' wedding. Asked if he had been nervous debating **Jimmy Carter,** Reagan smiled, "No, not at all. I've been on the same stage with John Wayne."

- In one of his films, *The Winning Team,* Reagan played Philadelphia Phillies pitcher Grover Cleveland Alexander. Thus a president played the role of a character with a president's name.

★ Conversely, an actor who was not a president but whose name consists of those of three presidents played the movie role of a president. Megastar Harrison Ford (there were two Presidents Harrison) played President James Marshall in the movie *Air Force One.* **Ronald Reagan** and Harrison Ford are joined in another way: Harrison Ford has starred in four Star Wars films, and Reagan was a staunch proponent of the Star Wars antimissile defense system.

★ **Theodore Roosevelt** was the first president to use the privately owned press to communicate frequently with the public. As such, he was the founder of the presidential press conference. One rainy day he looked out the window and saw a group of reporters manning their usual post by the White House gates. Their usual purpose was to question those entering and leaving the White House in order to gain leads for news stories. Seeing them wet, cold, and miserable, Roosevelt invited them in and ordered that a room be set aside for them. In doing so, he granted the press a status it had never before enjoyed and that it has never since relinquished.

- While TR's press conferences were usually one-way lectures, often while the president was under the blade of his barber's razor, **Woodrow Wilson** instituted the practice of holding regular press conferences open to all accredited reporters, not just ones handpicked by the president and his staff.

Unlike TR, he did not direct discussion and allowed reporters to ask their questions. These innovations reduced the power of the president over the news generated by presidential press conferences.

- **Warren Harding,** a former newspaperman himself, made the press conference an official duty of his administration.

- During his 1924 presidential campaign, reporters eagerly sought out **Calvin Coolidge.** "Have you any statement about the campaign?" asked one reporter. "No," answered Coolidge. "Can you tell us something about the world situation?" "No." "Any information about the world situation?" "No." As the disappointed reporters started to leave, Coolidge said solemnly:" "Now remember—don't quote me."

- **Franklin Roosevelt** conducted press conferences twice a week, every week—992 sessions—through wartime and personal illness.

- Reporters were so put off by **Dwight Eisenhower**'s habit of rambling in press conferences that one of them rewrote the Gettysburg Address in the meandering style that Ike might have delivered it. The parody begins: "I haven't checked these figures, but eighty-seven years ago, I think it was, a number of individuals organized a government setup here in this country. I believe it covered certain eastern areas, with the idea they were following up, based on a sort of national independence arrangement . . . ."

- After he had lost his bid for president in 1960 and for California governor in 1962, **Richard Nixon** lashed out: "But as I leave you, I want you to know—just think how much you're going to be missing. You won't have Nixon to kick around anymore because, gentlemen, this is my last press conference." It was not his last

press conference; he was elected and reelected president in 1968 and 1972.

- **John F. Kennedy** was the first president to conduct press conferences on live television.

Jimmy Carter holding a press conference

- **Ronald Reagan** turned seventy in February 1981 and joked about his age in a speech to the Washington Press Club. "I know your organization was founded in 1919," he remarked. Then, after a slight pause, he added, "It seems like only yesterday."

★ As the twentieth century gathered momentum, radio became a significant medium through which to communicate the mind and heart of the presidency.

- **Warren Harding** was the first president to own a radio and the first to speak over the radio airwaves, with the aid of a long-distance wireless telephone.

- **Franklin Roosevelt**'s fireside chats were a series of thirty evening radio talks given between 1933 and 1944. Originally designed to garner support for his New Deal policies during the Great Depression, Roosevelt broadcast these evening radio talks to the American public straight from the White House. The addresses gave people a sense of hope and security during difficult times and helped keep Roosevelt popular despite the continuing

Franklin Roosevelt conducting one of his fireside chats, 1941

Depression. Because nearly every home in working-class neighborhoods had the radio on and windows open in summertime, it was possible to take a long walk without missing many of the president's words.

★ The assassination and funeral of **John F. Kennedy** marked a turning point in American history. It was the first time that virtually the entire nation came together to witness a national tragedy, and the witnessing was through

John F. Kennedy's funeral procession

television. The live coverage and images of those events—the shooting of Lee Harvey Oswald, the funeral cortege, the black-veiled widow, and the president's tiny son, John John, saluting the flag—seared the national psyche and established television as an archetypal source of news. Television has become, perhaps, the most powerful and pervasive medium during the past fifty years:

- **Herbert Hoover** appeared on the nation's first television broadcast in 1927, but as secretary of commerce, not as president.

- The first president to appear on television during his presidency was **Franklin Roosevelt.** He was seen by American viewers at the opening of the New York World's Fair on April 30, 1939.

- **Dwight Eisenhower** was the first president to appear on color television.

- The Kennedy-Nixon debates in 1960, watched by seventy million viewers, marked the grand entrance of television into presidential politics. Most experts credit **John F. Kennedy**'s successful TV-friendly performances in the four debates as a significant factor in his subsequent election. Tellingly, most polls indicated that **Richard Nixon** won the radio versions of those exchanges.

- During the first year, 1975–1976, of the cutting and cutting-edge television show *Saturday Night Live,* comedian Chevy Chase spoofed **Gerald Ford** by falling down a lot, and spectacularly. Chase's widely watched schtick was a takeoff on news footage that showed Ford stumbling on several occasions. **Jimmy Carter**'s razor-thin victory in 1976 over Ford, one of our nation's most athletic and fittest presidents, may have been significantly influenced by Chase depicting him as a stumblebum. Other *SNL* comedians who have spoofed presidents include Dan Aykroyd as **Jimmy Carter,** Phil Hartman as **Ronald Reagan,** Dana Carvey as **George H. W. Bush,** Darrell Hammond as **Bill Clinton,** Will Ferrell as **George W. Bush,** Fred Armisen as **Barack Obama,** and Alec Baldwin as **Donald Trump.**

- Many would support **Ronald Reagan** as our most television-savvy president. In his 1980 debates with **Jimmy Carter,** Reagan, at the end of the exchange, made sure to walk across the dais to shake hands with Carter—to show that Reagan was clearly the taller, and hence the more commanding, of the two. In his 1984 televised presidential debate against his considerably younger opponent, Walter Mondale, Reagan quipped, "I will not make age an issue in this campaign. I am not going to exploit, for political purposes, my opponent's youth and inexperience."

John F. Kennedy and Richard Nixon at televised debate, 1960

MORE FASCINATING
FACTS
ABOUT
OUR PRESIDENTS

★ ★ ★ ★

George and Martha Washington

THE CURTISS CANDY COMPANY claimed that its Baby Ruth candy bar, put on the market in 1921, was named after Ruth Cleveland, daughter of **Grover Cleveland.** In fact, although never proved in a court of law, the confection played off the name of baseball slugger Babe Ruth. Naming a candy bar after the long-dead daughter of a long-ago president—a daughter who died at the age of thirteen from diphtheria in 1904—would have been a bizarre choice.

That a candy bar named Baby Ruth appeared on the market just when a baseball player named Babe Ruth was becoming the most famous person in America raises our collective eyebrow even higher. Ironically, when a candy-making competitor secured Babe Ruth's permission to manufacture a confection named the "Babe Ruth Home Run Bar," Curtiss successfully sued to have the bar barred because the name too closely resembled that of their own product! So the Babe never collected a penny for either clump of candy.

Years later, the same Babe Ruth was asked by a reporter how the star slugger could demand an $80,000 annual salary when **Herbert Hoover** was making only $75,000. Ruth replied, "I know, but I had a better year than Hoover."

Those are the kinds of colorful and quirky facts about presidents that fail to make it into the pages of our textbooks. Here are some more tidbits of presidential trivia that you may not have learned in your high school or college American history courses:

★ **George Washington** and most of his contemporaries spoke with a British accent.

★ While Congress wished to address him as "His Highness, the President of the United States of America and the Protector of Their Liberties," **George**

Washington opted for, and established the tradition of, "Mr. President."

★ As the American minister to France, Benjamin Franklin attended a diplomatic dinner shortly after the American Revolutionary War ended. The French foreign minister opened the dinner by offering a champagne toast to his king: "To His Majesty, Louis the Sixteenth, who, like the moon, fills the earth with a soft, benevolent glow." The British ambassador then rose to give his toast: "To George the Third, who like the sun at noonday, spreads his light and illumines the world." Then the aging Franklin exulted: "I cannot give you the sun or the moon, but I give you **George Washington,** General of the Armies of the United States, who, like Joshua of old, commanded both the sun and the moon to stand still, and both obeyed!"

★ **John Adams** was the great-great-grandson of John and Priscilla Alden, pilgrims who landed at Plymouth Rock in 1620.

★ Carved into the mantelpiece of the State Dining Room in the White House are **John Adams**'s words:

I Pray Heaven To Bestow
The Best Of Blessings On
This House
And All That Shall Hereafter
Inhabit it
May none but Honest and
Wise Men ever rule
under This Roof.

★ When **Thomas Jefferson** took office in 1801, there were almost 900,000 slaves in a population of about 5,500,000 Americans. Jefferson owned approximately 200 slaves. Jefferson died $107,000 in debt, a defect partially alleviated by the sale of his slaves.

★ **Thomas Jefferson** was the principal founder of the Library of Congress. **Millard Fillmore** and his cabinet helped fight the Library of Congress fire of 1851, which destroyed the majority of the collection, many donated by or bought from Jefferson.

★ **Thomas Jefferson** was the first American to introduce french fried potatoes at a dinner party.

★ In 1803, **Thomas Jefferson** arranged the Louisiana Purchase, in which the United States almost doubled its land mass. The price: $15 million. Despite the lack of constitutional authority, Jefferson executed this bold feat without the consent of Congress.

★ **John Quincy Adams** argued before the Supreme Court on behalf of slaves from the ship *Amistad* who mutinied during their journey from Africa.

★ A telegram informing **Zachary Taylor** that he had been nominated for the presidency by the Whig Party was returned by the mail service. Taylor learned of the nomination in the newspaper.

★ **Millard Fillmore** refused an honorary degree from Oxford University because he felt he had "neither literary nor scientific attainment." He added

that no one should accept a degree that he couldn't actually read.

★ **Franklin Pierce** won the presidency by defeating his old commanding officer from the Mexican War, Winfield Scott.

★ **Abraham Lincoln** was defeated for the state legislature, failed in business, suffered a nervous breakdown, was defeated for nomination for

Zahary Taylor

Millard Fillmore

Congress, was rejected for land officer, was defeated as a candidate for the Senate, was defeated for nomination for vice president—and then became president.

★ **Andrew Johnson** is buried beneath a willow tree that he planted. As he requested, his head rests on a copy of the Constitution.

★ **Ulysses S. Grant,** so powerfully associated with the mass slaughters of the Civil War, was nauseated at the sight of blood, disliked hunting, abhorred cruelty to animals, and was sickened by the spectacle of a bullfight in Mexico.

★ During his term of office, **Ulysses S. Grant** was once arrested and fined $20 for exceeding the Washington speed limit on his horse. When the embarrassed policeman realized that he was dealing with the president, he hesitated to issue the ticket. But President Grant insisted on paying the fine and wrote a letter to the Washington Police Department commending the officer on his fine sense of duty.

★ "Who is buried in Grant's Tomb?" You may think that you know the answer to that old question, which Groucho Marx popularized on his quiz show *You Bet Your Life,* to ensure that each contestant won at least fifty dollars. But even visitors who are standing inside the magnificent monument often answer the riddle incorrectly. In a remote corner of bustling New York City, on a quiet bluff along the Hudson River far from Times

Square and Broadway, **Ulysses S. Grant** and his wife, Julia Dent, lie in a stately marble mausoleum. The monument was dedicated on the president's seventy-fifth birthday, April 27, 1897, almost twelve years after he had died. Five years later, his wife passed and was put to rest next to him. So you might think the answer to Groucho's question "Who is buried in Grant's Tomb?" would be "President and Mrs. Grant." Wrong again. The actual answer to the famous poser is that nobody is buried in Grant's Tomb. The Grants are *entombed* therein, not buried.

★ QUICK: Can you name six presidents who are not buried in the United States? As of the publication of this book, the six are *chuckle, chuckle, snort* **Jimmy Carter, George H. W. Bush, Bill Clinton, George W. Bush, Barack Obama,** and **Donald Trump.**

★ The famous detective Allan Pinkerton was a son-in-law of **Chester Arthur.**

★ **Theodore Roosevelt** was concerned that many young men were being severely injured, and in some cases killed, as a result of the rough and violent new contact sport called football. He petitioned to have the game banned in the United States, but the sport was too popular. As a result of his efforts, however, new rules were adopted and safety gear such as helmets were encouraged.

Allan Pinkerton

★ **Grover Cleveland** dedicated the Statue of Liberty on October 28, 1886.

★ **Calvin Coolidge,** a man of few words, was so famous for saying so little that a White House dinner guest made a bet that she could get the president to say more than two words. She told the president of her wager. His reply: "You lose."

★ **Herbert Hoover** was the youngest member of the first graduating class from Stanford University. He was treasurer of the junior class, the only elected office he held before assuming the presidency.

★ **Herbert Hoover** claimed that he never violated Prohibition, but he would regularly stop at the Belgian Embassy for a quick martini. The practice was legal since the embassy was considered foreign territory and not within the jurisdiction of the American government.

★ **Herbert Hoover** donated his entire presidential salary to charity.

★ According to *Presidential Doodles* (Basic Books, 2006), **Herbert Hoover** was the most artistic and productive doodler among our chief executives.

★ Anticipating a victory for **Harry Truman**'s opponent, Thomas E. Dewey, the *Chicago Daily Tribune* printed the headline DEWEY DEFEATS TRUMAN on the front page of its 1948 postelection edition— but Truman won. Stunned by his defeat, Dewey sighed that he felt like the man who woke up to find himself inside a coffin with a lily in his hand and thought, "If I'm alive, what am I doing here? And if I'm dead, why do I have to go to the bathroom?"

★ A graduate of West Point, **Dwight Eisenhower** was the last U.S. general (and the only one in the twentieth century) to become president. In World War II he was in charge of the D-Day invasion in 1944 and served as

Monticello

commander in chief of the Allies in Europe. He had previously served as a commissioned officer in World War I. His parents were members of a fundamentalist religious sect and were strict pacifists.

★ **Dwight Eisenhower** played football at West Point and was injured trying to tackle Olympic and NFL star Jim Thorpe.

★ **Dwight Eisenhower** changed the name of the presidential retreat in the Maryland hills from Shangri-La to Camp David, after his grandson.

★ In 1962, **John F. Kennedy** entertained a group of Nobel Prize winners at

the White House. Chalice in hand, Kennedy rose to toast the luminaries in the room. He heralded the event as "the most distinguished gathering of intellectual talent ever brought together in the Executive Mansion—except for when **Thomas Jefferson** dined alone." In addition to Jefferson's political contributions, described throughout this book, our third president designed many of the first buildings of the University of Virginia, which he founded, and two of his other architectural designs— Monticello and Bremo—are still among the most exquisite country houses in America. He had much to do with the planning of Washington, DC, and invented early versions of the swivel chair, collapsible writing table, and the pedometer, to measure his walks.

★ In the family of **Lyndon Baines Johnson,** everybody had to have the same initials: wife Lady Bird Johnson (her real name was Claudia), daughters Luci Baines Johnson and Lynda Bird

Johnson, and the family dog, Little Beagle Johnson.

★ **Lyndon Johnson** and his wife, Lady Bird, held a Festival of the Arts at the White House, the first of its kind. At the festival, Sarah Vaughan, the great jazz singer, held her distinguished audience rapt for a half hour. As the party was breaking up, a White House staffer found Miss Vaughan weeping in her dressing room. "What's the matter?" asked the staffer. "Nothing is the matter," said the singer. "It's just that twenty years ago, when I came to Washington, I couldn't even get a hotel room. But tonight, I sang for the president of the United States—and then he asked me to dance with him. It is more than I can stand."

★ **Richard Nixon** received a gold-plated .45-caliber pistol as a gift from Elvis Presley.

★ When he received his commission in 1943, **George H. W. Bush** became, at 19, the youngest pilot then in the U.S. Navy. He flew fifty-eight combat missions during World War II. He romantically painted the name "Barbara" on the side of his bomber.

★ The daughter of the author of this book was fired on national television by an American president. That's right. On the last day of the 2009 season of the reality television show Celebrity Apprentice, **Donald Trump** fired my daughter, poker champion Annie Duke, in favor of comedienne Joan Rivers.

Richard Nixon and Elvis Presley in the Oval Office, 1970

INAUGURATIONS:
OMENS OF
THINGS TO COME

★ ★ ★ ★

Abraham Lincoln taking the oath of office at his second inauguration, 1865

THE STORY BEHIND the word *inaugurate* is an intriguing one. It literally means "to take omens from the flight of birds." In ancient Rome, augurs would predict the outcome of an enterprise by the way the birds were flying. These soothsayer-magicians would tell a general whether or not to march or to do battle by the formations of the birds on the wing. They might even catch one and cut it open to observe its entrails for omens.

Nowadays, presidential candidates use their inauguration speeches to take flight on an updraft of words, rather than birds—and they do often spill their guts for all to see. It all began with **George Washington,** whose first inaugural began this way: "Among the vicissitudes incident to life, no event could have filled me with greater anxieties than that of which the notification was transmitted by your order, and received on the fourteenth day of the present month. On the one hand, I was summoned by my country, whose voice I can never hear but with veneration and love, from a retreat which I had chosen with the fondest predilection, and, in my flattering hopes, with an immutable decision, as the asylum of my declining years."

The shortest inauguration speech of all American presidents, only 133 words, was delivered by **George Washington** at his second inaugural on March 4, 1793. **Abraham Lincoln**'s second inaugural address was the second shortest.

The longest inauguration address, delivered by **William Henry Harrison** on March 4, 1841, contained 8,445 words.

Washington's speech lasted about two minutes; Harrison's speech took about an hour and forty-five minutes to deliver.

The fact that the longest speech preceded the shortest presidential term in American history was no coincidence. Harrison delivered his message outdoors, on the east portico of the Capitol. In spite of the chilly, rainy, and snowy day, Harrison refused to wear a hat, scarf, overcoat, or gloves.

(Having studied medicine for a year at the University of Pennsylvania, Harrison should have known better.) After his address, Harrison attended a round of receptions in his damp clothing and caught a cold that developed into pneumonia, from which he died in the White House on April 4, 1841, a scant thirty-one days after he had been sworn in. As a result, Harrison's lack of brevity and lack of longevity are the only enduring marks left on his presidential legacy. Moral: Wear your galoshes and keep your speeches short.

Here are some inaugural firsts:

★ **George Washington** set the precedents of kissing the Bible after the oath and of presenting an inaugural speech. His was written primarily by **James Madison.**

★ **John Adams** was the first president to receive the oath from the chief justice of the United States (Oliver Ellsworth). No chief justice has ever missed a presidential swearing-in ceremony.

★ **Thomas Jefferson** was the first president to be inaugurated at the Capitol in Washington, DC.

★ The first inaugural ball was held for **James Madison.**

★ In 1817, the inauguration of **James Monroe** was the first to be held

James Monroe

outdoors. Monroe became the first to give an inaugural address to an assembled public crowd. Since that time, the traditional inaugural address has been an opportunity for the president to speak directly to the American people.

★ **Martin Van Buren**'s inauguration marked the first time that outgoing and incoming presidents (**Andrew Jackson** and Van Buren) rode together in a carriage to the Capitol for the event. Two other memorable rides through the Washington streets occurred:

- In 1921, outgoing President **Woodrow Wilson** and incoming President **Warren Harding** took the inaugural ride together. Both men raised their hats and waved to the cheering crowds. On this greatest day of his life, people-person Harding wanted to wave to every soul on earth. But he noticed that the waving caused considerable pain to the stroke-afflicted Wilson.

Harding stopped waving so that the debilitated Wilson could also stop.

- Probably the most uncomfortable pairing of outgoing and incoming presidents was in 1933, when **Herbert Hoover,** depressed by the Depression, and **Franklin Roosevelt** rode together to Roosevelt's inauguration. The gloomy Hoover sat in silence, knowing that the adoring crowds were cheering optimistically not at all for him, but for his dashing successor.

★ **James Polk**'s inauguration was the first to be reported by telegraph.

★ **Franklin Pierce** was the first president to memorize his inaugural address—a 3,319-word speech that he delivered without the aid of notes.

★ **James Buchanan**'s inauguration was the first to be photographed.

* **Abraham Lincoln**'s second inauguration marked the first time that African Americans participated in the inaugural parade.

* **Ulysses S. Grant** was the first president whose father and mother were alive at the time of his inauguration. **John F. Kennedy** and **George W. Bush** were also fortunate enough to have both parents live long enough to see them become president, and their parents actually attended the ceremonies.

* **James Garfield**'s mother was the first to attend her son's inauguration.

* **William McKinley**'s 1901 inauguration was the first to appear in a newsreel. Six months later, we has assassinated.

* The inaugurations of **William Howard Taft,** in 1909, and **Ronald Reagan,** in 1985, had to be moved indoors at the Capitol, because of frigid weather.

* **William Howard Taft**'s inauguration was the first time that a president's wife rode with her husband in the procession from the Capitol to the White House.

* **Woodrow Wilson**'s inauguration was the first time that women participated in the inaugural parade.

* **Warren Harding** was the first president to ride to and from his inauguration in an automobile.

* **Harry Truman**'s inauguration was the first to be televised.

William Howard Taft and Theodore Roosevelt riding to inauguration, 1909

★ **John F. Kennedy**'s inauguration marked the first time a poet, Robert Frost, participated in the official ceremonies at the Capitol. **Bill Clinton** was the only other president to feature poets at his inauguration— Maya Angelou at his first and Miller Williams at his second.

★ **Jimmy Carter** was the first president sworn in by his nickname. His Inauguration Day parade featured a giant peanut-shaped balloon.

★ The inauguration of **Ronald Reagan** was the biggest, fanciest, and costliest in American history. Comedian Johnny Carson observed wryly, "This is the first administration to have a premiere."

★ Forty million jelly beans were consumed at **Ronald Reagan**'s inaugural, almost the number of votes he received in the election.

★ **Bill Clinton**'s inaugural was the first to be broadcast live on the Internet and

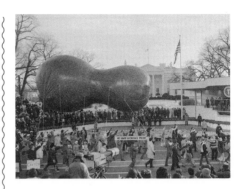

Peanut-shaped balloon at Jimmy Carter's inauguration

the first to fall on the Martin Luther King Jr. holiday.

QUICK: Name a president who did not deliver an inaugural address.

Actually, you have a choice of five. Presidents **John Tyler, Millard Fillmore, Andrew Johnson, Chester Arthur,** and **Gerald Ford** did not deliver inaugural speeches because they were never elected to the presidency.

Here are some more inaugural onlys and oddities:

★ On what month and day do we move ahead with vigor? The answer is March fourth! And it was on that very day that our presidents from **John Adams** to **Franklin Roosevelt** were inaugurated. Except for **George Washington**'s first inaugural, when he was sworn in on April 30, 1789, all presidents until 1939 were inaugurated on March 4 in an effort to avoid bad weather. Washington's inauguration was more than a month late because Congress had not properly convened, so his first term was that much shorter than his second. The Twentieth Amendment changed the inauguration date to January 20. **Franklin Roosevelt**'s second inauguration was the first to be held on that date.

★ The words that everyone waits to hear from their new leader are: "I do solemnly swear that I will faithfully execute the office of the president of the United States, and will to the best of my ability, preserve, protect, and defend the Constitution of the United States."

★ Both Adamses, father and son, made it a point to leave Washington the day before their successors' inaugurations.

★ **Thomas Jefferson** was the only president to walk to and from his inauguration.

★ Colorful **Andrew Jackson** invited any and all of his fellow Tennesseeans to his inauguration party at the White House. "It was like the inundation of the northern barbarians into Rome," wrote one eyewitness, "save that the tumultuous tide came in from a different point of the compass. The West and the South seemed to have precipitated themselves upon the North and overwhelmed it." Ruffians knocked the trays out of waiters' hand, smashed china and glassware, overturned furniture, brushed bric-a-brac from mantels, spilled whiskey and chicken and spat tobacco juice on the carpets, and stood with muddy boots on damask-covered chairs to get a good look at "Old Hickory." The festivities got so out of hand, including extensive monetary damage to the furnishings, that the president left the party and spent the night at a Washington hotel.

★ In at least one way, **Zachary Taylor** became the darling of trivia buffs. In March 1849 he refused to be inaugurated and take the oath of office on a Sunday because of his religious beliefs. The offices of president and vice president were vacant at the time, so someone had to be the president, but who? David Rice Atchison, the president pro tempore of the Senate, was sworn in as president. He didn't do much. When asked what he did that day, he said, "I went to bed. There had been two or three busy nights finishing up the work of the Senate, and I slept most of that Sunday."

★ **Franklin Pierce**'s eleven-year-old son was killed in a train crash as the family traveled toward the inauguration. The boy was the only fatality.

★ **James Buchanan** was the only president to announce in his inaugural

James Buchanan

address that he would not run for reelection.

★ In 1861, with our nation on the brink of war and rumors of assassination swirling, **Abraham Lincoln** had to travel undercover and slip into Washington undetected.

★ **Rutherford B. Hayes** was the first president to take the oath of office in the White House. Afraid of violent disruption at a public inauguration after the most contentious election in American history, President **Ulysses S. Grant** invited Hayes to the White House, where he was administered the oath of office in the Red Room. Democrats boycotted the inauguration.

★ **Chester Arthur** took the oath of office in his own home.

★ At his inauguration in 1905, **Theodore Roosevelt** wore a ring, inside of which was a lock of **Abraham Lincoln**'s hair. Roosevelt was a great admirer of Lincoln, and as a child had watched Lincoln's funeral procession pass by his home.

★ In 1923, upon the death of President Harding, **Calvin Coolidge** was sworn in by his father, a notary public. The elder Coolidge read the oath of office to his son by the light of a kerosene lamp in the parlor of a remote Vermont farmhouse. In 1925, Coolidge was administered the oath of office by

Rutherford B. Hayes

an ex-president, **William Howard Taft,** who was then chief justice of the Supreme Court. Coolidge's inauguration was also the first to be broadcast nationally by radio. **Herbert Hoover** was also sworn in by Chief Justice Taft, in 1929.

★ After his inauguration ceremonies on March 4, 1933, **Franklin Roosevelt** immediately went into action. On that same day, his cabinet was nominated, accepted, sworn in, and called into session, the only time that has happened.

★ **Lyndon Johnson**'s inauguration was the only time that the oath was administered in an airplane (Air Force One, a Boeing 707, at Love Field in Dallas, Texas) and the only time that the oath was administered by a woman, Sarah T. Hughes, U. S. district judge of the Northern District of Texas. Johnson and **Ronald Reagan** were the only

Judge Sarah T. Hughes swearing in President Lyndon B. Johnson on Air Force One

presidents to be sworn in with their wives holding the Bible.

★ After hearing **John F. Kennedy**'s inaugural address, **Richard Nixon** remarked to Ted Sorensen, a Kennedy aide, "I wish I had said some of those things." "What part?" Sorensen wanted to know. "The part about 'ask what your country can do for you . . .'?" "No," said Nixon. "The part that starts, 'I do solemnly swear.'"

★ The warmest January inauguration on record was **Ronald Reagan**'s first: 55 degrees; the coldest his second: 7 degrees.

Here are statements culled from the inaugural addresses of some twentieth-century American presidents. Identify each president.

1. We are provincials no longer. The tragic events of the thirty months of vital turmoil through which we have just passed have made us citizens of the world. There can be no turning back. Our own

John F. Kennedy's inauguration

fortunes as a nation are involved whether we would have it so or not.

2. There would be little traffic in illegal liquor if only criminals patronized it. We must awake to the fact that this patronage from large numbers of law-abiding citizens is supplying the rewards and stimulating crime.

3. First of all, let me assert my firm belief that the only thing we have to fear is fear itself—nameless, unreasoning, unjustified terror which paralyzes needed efforts to convert retreat into advance.

4. And so, my fellow Americans: Ask not what your country can do for you—ask what you can do for your country.

5. Now, so there will be no misunderstanding, it's not my intention to do away with government. It is rather to make it work with us, not over us; to stand by our side, not ride on our back. Government can and must provide opportunity, not smother it; foster productivity, not stifle it.

ANSWERS

1. *Woodrow Wilson*
2. *Herbert Hoover*
3. *Franklin Roosevelt*
4. *John F. Kennedy*
5. *Ronald Reagan*

WHAT'S IN A
PRESIDENT'S
NAME?

★ ★ ★ ★

Grover Cleveland's first name was Stephen

SEVEN OF OUR AMERICAN presidents had their names legally changed between birth and prominence:

★ **Ulysses S. Grant** came into this world as Hiram Ulysses Grant. When his name was mistakenly entered on the West Point register as *Ulysses S. Grant* (the *S.* was for Simpson, his mother's maiden name), he eagerly embraced the error because he detested the initials *H.U.G.* and loved having the initials *U.S.*, as in "United States," "Uncle Sam," and "Unconditional Surrender."

★ Which president was born a king? Born Leslie Lynch King Jr., **Gerald R. Ford Jr.** took the name of his adoptive father after his mother's divorce. Similarly, **William Jefferson Clinton** was born William Jefferson Blythe III, three months after his father died in an automobile accident. When his mother wed Roger Clinton, he took the family name.

★ Less pyrotechnically, Grover was originally the birth-certificate middle name of Stephen **Grover Cleveland,** Woodrow the middle name of Thomas **Woodrow Wilson,** Calvin the middle name of John **Calvin Coolidge,** and Dwight the middle name of David **Dwight Eisenhower.**

Leslie Lynch King Jr. became Gerald R. Ford Jr.

AN ANAGRAM IS THE REARRANGEMENT of all the letters in a word or phrase to create another word or phrase. Here are the best efforts to anagram the names of our twentieth- and twenty-first-century presidents. Some work better grammatically than others, some are more appropriate to the president, some less telling.

THEODORE ROOSEVELT	LOVED HORSE; TREE, TOO.
WILLIAM HOWARD TAFT	A WORD WITH ALL: I'M FAT.
WOODROW WILSON	O LORD, SO NOW WWI.
WARREN GAMALIEL HARDING	REAL WINNER? HIM A LAGGARD.
CALVIN COOLIDGE	LOVE? A COLD ICING.
HERBERT CLARK HOOVER	O, HARK, CLEVER BROTHER.
FRANKLIN DELANO ROOSEVELT	ELEANOR, KIN, LAST FOND LOVER
HARRY S. TRUMAN	RASH ARMY RUNT
DWIGHT DAVID EISENHOWER	HE DID VIEW THE WAR DOINGS.
JOHN FITZGERALD KENNEDY	ZING! JOY DARKEN, THEN FLED.
LYNDON BAINES JOHNSON	NO NINNY, HE'S ON JOB LADS.
RICHARD MILHOUS NIXON	HUSH—NIX CRIMINAL ODOR!
GERALD RUDOLPH FORD	A RUDER LORD; GOLF PH.D
JAMES EARL CARTER	A RARE, CALM JESTER
RONALD W. REAGAN	A WAN OLD RANGER
GEORGE BUSH	HE BUGS GORE.
WILLIAM JEFFERSON CLINTON	JILTS NICE WOMEN; IN FOR FALL
GEORGE W. BUSH	HE GREW BOGUS / WE GUSH OR BEG.
BARACK HUSSEIN OBAMA	ABRAHAM IS BACK. ONE U.S.!
DONALD TRUMP	DUMP TAN LORD

What is the most popular first name among presidents? The answer is *James*. Six presidents share that first name—Madison, Monroe, Polk, Buchanan, Garfield, and Carter. Tied for second place are *William* with four—Harrison, McKinley, Taft, and Clinton—and *John* with four—Adams, Quincy Adams, Tyler, and Kennedy. Massachusetts is the birth state of three presidents named John—Adams, Quincy Adams, and Kennedy. In 2004, Senator John Kerry failed in his bid to become the fourth.

Despite fourteen presidents with the first names James, John, and William, twenty of our chief executives, starting with **Thomas Jefferson** and ending with **Donald Trump,** have first names not shared by any other man in the office.

Five pairs of presidents have shared the same last name—*Adams, Harrison, Johnson, Roosevelt,* and *Bush.* Only the Johnsons were unrelated to each other.

Here are some other letter-perfect tidbits of presidential nomenclature:

Donald Trump

★ Five presidential last names consist of four letters. In chronological order, they are *Polk, Taft, Ford, Bush,* and *Bush.* **George W. Bush** is the only one among them to serve two terms.

★ In contrast to the monosyllabic monikers above, *Eisenhower* is the only presidential surname that contains four syllables.

★ Three presidents' first names begin with a vowel, the letter *A*—**Andrew Jackson, Abraham Lincoln,** and **Andrew Johnson.**

★ *Obama* is the only presidential surname that begins and ends with a vowel.

★ *H* is the most popular first letter of presidential surnames—**William Henry Harrison, Rutherford B. Hayes, Benjamin Harrison, Warren Harding,** and **Herbert Hoover.** *S* is the most common letter at the beginning of English words, but no president's surname starts with that letter.

★ Only one president's name contains a letter that is found in no other president's name. That letter is the *Q* in **John Quincy Adams.**

★ **Ulysses Simpson Grant** and **Rutherford Birchard Hayes** are the

only presidential names that contain *a, e, i, o,* and *u,* with a *y* to boot.

★ Four presidents have had alliterative first and last names—**Woodrow Wilson, Calvin Coolidge, Herbert Hoover,** and **Ronald Reagan.** They all served in the twentieth century.

Herbert Hoover

★ The letters *J* and *T* start the last names of nine presidents—**Thomas Jefferson, Andrew Jackson, Andrew Johnson,** and **Lyndon Johnson,** and **John Tyler, Zachary Taylor, William Howard Taft, Harry Truman,** and **Donald Trump.**

Andrew Johnson

★ Pierce, Grant, Ford, Bush, Trump, and (in Britain) Hoover are all common English words when uncapitalized.

PRESIDENTIAL
NICKNAMES

★ ★ ★ ★

Richard Nixon on the campaign trail in Paoli, Pennsylvania, 1968

Theodore Roosevelt (he roundly disliked the nickname "Teddy") was our initial president to be identified at times by his initials, *TR*. FDR, JFK, and LBJ followed TR's lead.

A more famous set of initials was attached to an earlier president.

In the 1830s, in New England, there was a craze for initialisms, in the manner of *FYI, PDQ, aka,* and *TGIF,* so popular today. The fad went so far as to generate letter combinations of intentionally comic misspellings: *KG* for "know go," *KY* for "know yuse," *NSMJ* for "'nough said 'mong jentlemen," and *OR* for "oll rong." *OK* for "oll correct" naturally followed.

Of all those loopy initialisms and facetious misspellings, *OK* alone survived. That's because of a presidential nickname that consolidated the letters in the national memory. **Martin Van Buren,** elected our eighth president in 1836, was born in Kinderhook, New York, and early in his political career was dubbed

"Old Kinderhook." Echoing the "Oll Korrect" initialism, *OK* became the rallying cry of the Old Kinderhook Club, a Democratic organization supporting Van Buren during the 1840 campaign. Thus the accident of Van Buren's birthplace rescued *OK* from the dustbin of history.

The coinage did Van Buren no good, and he was defeated in his bid for reelection. But the word honoring his name today remains what H. L. Mencken identified as "the most shining and successful Americanism ever invented."

Martin Van Buren's home in Kinderhook, New York

Match the following presidential nicknames in the left-hand column with the presidents in the right-hand column:

1. The Great Emancipator
2. Old Hickory
3. The Father of His Country
4. The Sage of Monticello
5. Ike
6. The King of Camelot
7. Tricky Dicky
8. Silent Cal
9. Tippecanoe
10. Unconditional Surrender
11. Old Rough and Ready
12. The Gipper
13. The New Dealer
14. The Schoolmaster
15. The Rough Rider
16. Big Bill
17. The Bachelor President
18. The Haberdasher

a. James Buchanan
b. Calvin Coolidge
c. Dwight Eisenhower
d. Ulysses S. Grant
e. William Henry Harrison
f. Andrew Jackson
g. Thomas Jefferson
h. John F. Kennedy
i. Abraham Lincoln
j. Richard Nixon
k. Ronald Reagan
l. Franklin Roosevelt
m. Theodore Roosevelt
n. William Howard Taft
o. Zachary Taylor
p. Harry Truman
q. George Washington
r. Woodrow Wilson

ANSWERS

1. i ★ 2. f ★ 3. q ★ 4. g★ 5. c ★ 6. h ★ 7. j ★ 8.b ★ 9. e ★ 10. d ★ 11. o ★ 12.k ★ 13. l ★ 14. r ★ 15. m ★ 16. n ★ 17. a ★ 18. p

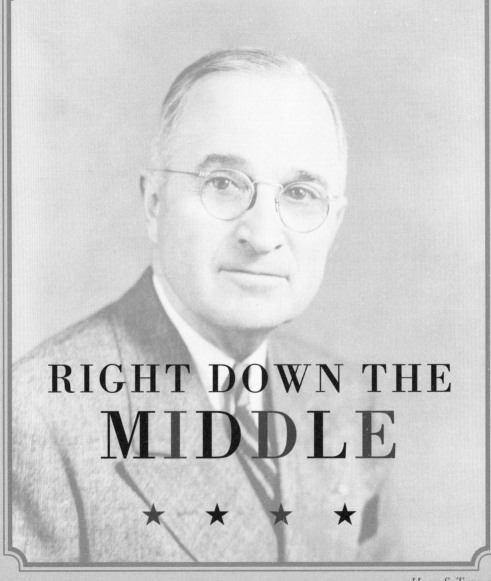

RIGHT DOWN THE
MIDDLE

★ ★ ★ ★

Harry S. Truman

PRESIDENTS HAVE MORE than their share of intriguing middle names.

Two of them—**Ronald *Wilson* Reagan** and **William *Jefferson* Clinton**—match the last names of two of their predecessors.

And then there's **Harry S. Truman**—or is it Harry S Truman, without the period? Truman initiated this punctuation controversy in 1962, when he told reporters that the *S* wasn't an initial for a particular name. Rather, the *S* was a compromise between the names of his grandfathers, Anderson Shipp Truman and Solomon Young, making the letter a kind of embracive middle name.

But Truman himself usually placed a period after the *S,* and the most authoritative style manuals recommend its use in the interest of consistency, even if the initial does not appear to stand for any particular name.

Using each middle name listed below, identify the full name of each American president:

1. Abram
2. Alan
3. Baines
4. Birchard
5. Clark
6. Delano
7. Earl
8. Fitzgerald
9. Gamaliel
10. Henry
11. Herbert Walker
12. Howard
13. Knox
14. Milhous
15. Quincy
16. Walker

ANSWERS

1. James Abram Garfield
2. Chester Alan Arthur
3. Lyndon Baines Johnson
4. Rutherford Birchard Hayes
5. Herbert Clark Hoover
6. Franklin Delano Roosevelt
7. James Earl Carter
8. John Fitzgerald Kennedy
9. Warren Gamaliel Harding
10. William Henry Harrison
11. George Herbert Walker Bush
12. William Howard Taft
13. James Knox Polk
14. Richard Milhous Nixon
15. John Quincy Adams
16. George Walker Bush

WHAT IT TAKES
TO BE
PRESIDENT

★ ★ ★ ★

AMERICAN PRESIDENTS have frequently commented on the joys and vicissitudes of their job. Judging by the utterances of some of our earliest chief executives, they did not take kindly to the position:

★ "My movements to the chair of government," lamented **George Washington** in a letter, "will be accompanied by feelings not unlike those of a culprit who is going to the place of his execution."

★ "No man who ever held the office of president would congratulate a friend on obtaining it," added **John Adams.**

★ "No man will ever bring out of the presidency the reputation which carries him into it. To myself, personally, it brings nothing but increasing drudgery and daily loss of friends," sighed **Thomas Jefferson,** who called the office "a splendid misery."

★ The second Adams, **John Quincy Adams,** echoed his father's disaffection with the office: "The four most miserable years of my life were my four years in the presidency."

★ **Martin Van Buren** shrugged, "As to the presidency, the two happiest days of my life were those of my entrance upon the office and my surrender of it."

★ **Harry Truman** complained, "Being a president is like riding a tiger. A man has to keep on riding or be swallowed."

★ **Lyndon Johnson** employed a different animal simile: "Being president is like being a jackass in a hailstorm. There's nothing to do but to stand there and take it."

★ Because of the Civil War, **James Buchanan** believed he would be the last president of the United States. Buchanan told **Abraham Lincoln,** "My dear, sir, if you are as happy on entering the White House as I on leaving, you are a very happy man indeed."

★ **Abraham Lincoln** may have said it best. When asked how it felt to be president, he explained: "You have heard about the man tarred and feathered and ridden out of town on a rail? A man in the audience asked him how he liked it, and his reply was that if it wasn't for the honor of the thing, he would much rather walk."

Later presidents have not been so dark in their assessments:

★ "When you get to be president, there are all those things, the honors, the twenty-one gun salutes, all those things. You have to remember it isn't for you. It's for the presidency," observed **Harry Truman,** whose most famous words about the office were "The buck stops here."

★ **Ronald Reagan** smiled and said, "When I was announcing sports, I was happy and thought that was all I wanted out of life. Then came the chance at Hollywood, and that was even better. Now I'm doing something that makes everything else I've done seem dull as dishwater when I look back."

★ **Bill Clinton** was able to extract humor from his two terms in office: "Being president is like running a cemetery: You've got a lot of people under you, and nobody's listening." "No president has ever enjoyed himself as much as I have enjoyed myself!"

Tombstones at Arlington National Cemetery

★ **Theodore Roosevelt** yawped, "While president, I have been president emphatically!"

Many nonpresidents have offered their wisdom about the presidency:

★ I would rather be right than president.—*Henry Clay*

Ted Kennedy

★ Frankly, I don't mind not being president. I just mind that someone else is.
—*Ted Kennedy*

★ The presidency we get is the country we get. With each new president the nation is conformed spiritually.
—*E. L. Doctorow*

★ The president's decisions make the weather, and if he is great enough, change the climate, too.
—*Theodore H. White*

★ They pick a president and then for four years they pick on him.
—*Adlai Stevenson*

★ *Presidency:* The greased pig in the field game of American politics.
—*Ambrose Bierce*

★ The presidency is now a cross between a popularity contest and a high school debate, with an encyclopaedia of clichés the first prize.—*Saul Bellow*

★ The office of the president is such a bastardizing thing, half royalty and half democracy, that nobody knows whether to genuflect or spit.—*Jimmy Breslin*

★ You can fool some of the people all of the time, and all the people some of the time, which is just long enough to be president of the United States.
—*Spike Milligan*

★ Any American who is prepared to run for president should automatically, by definition, be disqualified from ever doing so.—*Gore Vidal*

RUNNING
MATES

★ ★ ★ ★

CHESTER ARTHUR exulted that it was "a greater honor than I ever dreamed of attaining." Humorist Bill Vaughan called it "the last cookie on the plate. Everybody insists he won't take it, but somebody always does." They were talking about the vice presidency—that colorful, increasingly important, and routinely disparaged American political institution.

Theodore Roosevelt

Others have been more blunt. **John Adams,** our first vice president, described the position as "the most insignificant that ever the imagination of man contrived or his imagination conceived."

"The vice presidency isn't worth a pitcher of warm spit." That was the advice **John Nance Garner,** vice president under Franklin Roosevelt, gave to **Lyndon Johnson,** a fellow Texan who had been asked by John F. Kennedy in 1960 to be Kennedy's running mate. Johnson accepted the offer and became president when Kennedy was assassinated.

When asked if he might consider becoming vice president, war hero John McCain responded, "You know, I spent all those years in a North Vietnamese prison camp, kept in the dark, fed scraps—why the heck would I want to do that all over again?"

Under the original terms of the Constitution, the first vice presidents were the presidential candidates who placed second in the electoral college

John Nance Garner

voting for the office of president of the United States. Apparently, the signers of the Constitution believed that party politics would not interfere with the president and his vice president working together in exquisite harmony. Yeah, sure. In 1804, after a poisonous campaign between John Adams and his own vice president, **Thomas Jefferson,** the Twelfth Amendment required members of the Electoral College to vote separately for president and vice president.

Fourteen presidents have served as vice presidents—**John Adams, Thomas Jefferson, Martin Van Buren, John Tyler, Millard Fillmore, Andrew Johnson, Chester Arthur, Theodore Roosevelt, Calvin Coolidge, Harry Truman, Richard Nixon, Lyndon Johnson, Gerald Ford,** and **George H. W. Bush.**

You'd think, then, that a natural and common way to become president would be for a president and vice president to finish their terms naturally and for the vice president to run and win election as the next president.

In 1988, **George H. W. Bush** did just that, succeeding Ronald Reagan. But you have to go back more than 150 years to find a vice president who became president immediately after his president voluntarily stepped aside. That man was **Martin Van Buren.** In 1836, Van Buren was elected president immediately

following his term as vice president, under Andrew Jackson.

The only other vice president/president who fits this pattern is **John Adams,** who succeeded George Washington. All three of these vice presidents who turned president immediately after their vice presidency—Adams, Van Buren, and Bush—lost their bids for reelection as president for a second term.

Here are some more fascinating facts about our vice presidents:

★ For parts of their presidency or for their entire term, James Madison, Andrew Jackson, John Tyler, Millard Fillmore, Franklin Pierce, Andrew Johnson, Ulysses S. Grant, Theodore Roosevelt, Harry Truman, Lyndon Johnson, Richard Nixon, and Gerald Ford had no vice president.

★ **Aaron Burr,** Thomas Jefferson's first vice president, fought perhaps the most famous duel in American history. A bitter political rival of Alexander

Hamilton, Burr took umbrage at Hamilton's remarks at a dinner party. Burr challenged Hamilton to a duel and mortally wounded his rival in the exchange of gunfire. Burr was indicted for murder, and although the charges were ultimately dismissed, he was driven from political life and the vice presidency.

Alexander Hamilton and Aaron Burr duel, 1804

★ Can you think of the only other sitting vice president who shot a man? The answer is **Dick Cheney,** who, while shooting quail, accidentally peppered friend and attorney Harry Whittington with birdshot.

★ **Elbridge Gerry,** a vice president to James Madison, is eponymously responsible for inspiring a political term in our English language. In 1812, in an effort to sustain his party's power, Governor Gerry divided the state of Massachusetts into electoral districts with more regard to politics than to geographical reality. It happened that one of the governor's manipulated districts resembled a salamander. To a drawing of the district, Gilbert Stuart—the same fellow who had painted the famous portrait of George Washington—added a head, eyes, wings, and claws. According to one version of the story, Stuart exclaimed about his creation, "That looks like a salamander!" "No," riposted the editor of the newspaper in which the cartoon was to appear, "better call it a Gerrymander!" The name *gerrymander* (now lowercased and sounded with a soft *g*, even though Gerry's name began with a hard *g*) is still used today to describe the shaping of electoral entities for political gain.

★ Seven vice presidents died in office—**George Clinton, Elbridge Gerry, William King, Henry Wilson, Thomas Hendricks, Garret Hobart,** and **James Sherman.** Only one president had two vice presidents die during his time in office. James Madison served two terms, and both times the man elected as his vice president died shortly after the beginning of the term—first, **George Clinton** and second, **Elbridge Gerry.**

★ Two men have served as vice president under two different presidents—

John C. Calhoun

George Clinton (under Jefferson and Madison) and **John C. Calhoun** (Quincy Adams and Jackson).

★ Two men resigned their vice presidency—**John C. Calhoun,** in 1832, to take a seat in the Senate, and **Spiro Agnew,** in 1973, upon pleading no contest to charges of accepting bribes while governor of Maryland.

★ **John Tyler** was born in the same county as his president, William Henry Harrison—Charles City County, Virginia.

★ **William Rufus de Vane King,** vice president to Franklin Pierce, was sworn into office in Cuba, the only executive officer to take the oath on foreign soil. King had gone to Cuba to recuperate, unsuccessfully, from tuberculosis and severe alcoholism. He died in 1853 after being vice president for just twenty-five days.

★ **Calvin Coolidge** was the first vice president not to seek two full terms

Charles Dawes

after ascending to the presidency. **Harry Truman** and **Lyndon Johnson** were the only others.

★ **Charles Dawes,** vice president under Calvin Coolidge, composed a number of songs, including a well-known piece for violin, "Melody in A Minor," and the popular song "It's All in the Game." In 1925, Dawes received the Nobel Peace Prize for his chairmanship of the Allied Reparations Commission and his origination of the Dawes Plan

to facilitate Germany's payments of wartime debts.

★ **Charles Curtis,** Herbert Hoover's running mate, is the only vice president of Native American ancestry. His mother was one-quarter Kaw, and he spent part of his early life on a Kaw reservation. Curtis, a great-great-grandson of White Plume, a Kaw chief who had offered assistance to the Lewis and Clark Expedition in 1804, was the only

Charles Curtis

president or vice president of Native American descent. He was also the last vice president (or president) to sport facial hair, in this case a mustache, while in office.

★ Franklin Roosevelt is the only president to have had three vice presidents— **John Nance Garner, Henry Wallace, and Harry Truman.** FDR is also the only failed vice presidential candidate to have gone on to become president.

★ **Alben Barkley** coined the word *veep* to describe his position in the Truman administration.

★ **Richard Nixon** is the only man to serve twice as vice president and twice as president. Nixon completed his vice presidency in 1960 and was narrowly defeated by John F. Kennedy for the presidency. He was elected president eight years later. As such, he is the only vice president to become president after a gap between the two offices and the only twentieth-century president to win the office on his second try.

★ When John F. Kennedy was told that he would have no trouble garnering the Democratic nomination for vice president, he quipped, "Let's not talk so much about vice. I'm against vice in any form."

★ "Nattering nabobs of negativism" may be the best-known turn of phrase associated with a vice president. **Spiro Agnew,** who served under Richard Nixon and who had a particularly acrimonious relationship with the press, employed this term in 1970 to refer to the members of the media. He also deemed the Fourth Estate "an effete corps of impudent snobs."

★ In 2006, **Al Gore,** Bill Clinton's vice president, starred in an Oscar-winning documentary feature film, *An Inconvenient Truth,* about global warming. In 2007, Gore shared the Nobel Peace Prize for his contributions to the understanding of climate change.

The following vice presidents, listed alphabetically by last name, never became president. Identify the president under whom each served:

1. Alben Barkley
2. George M. Dallas
3. Hannibal Hamlin
4. Hubert Humphrey
5. Thomas R. Marshall
6. Richard Johnson
7. Walter Mondale
8. Dan Quayle
9. Nelson Rockefeller
10. Adlai Stevenson

Nelson Rockefeller

Adlai Stevenson

ANSWERS

1. Harry Truman
2. James Polk
3. Abraham Lincoln
4. Lyndon Johnson
5. Woodrow Wilson
6. Martin Van Buren
7. Jimmy Carter
8. George H. W. Bush
9. Gerald Ford
10. Grover Cleveland

FIRST LADIES
RULE

★ ★ ★ ★

Martha Washington

WHAT IS UNUSUAL about the following sentence?

FIRST LADIES RULE THE STATE
AND STATE THE RULE—
"LADIES FIRST!"

Perhaps you noticed that, when read forward and backward word by word, the sentence comes out the same.

Many early first ladies expressed their own preference for how they were addressed, including the use of such titles as "Lady," "Queen," "Mrs. President," and "Mrs. Presidentress." **Martha Dandridge Custis Washington** was often referred to as "Lady Washington."

In a eulogy at her funeral in 1849, President Zachary Taylor referred to **Dolley Madison** as "the first lady of the land for half a century." The title "First Lady" first gained nationwide recognition in 1877, when newspaper journalist Mary C. Ames referred to **Lucy Webb Hayes** as "the first lady of the land" while reporting on the inauguration of Rutherford B. Hayes. Lucy Hayes was a tremendously popular First Lady, and the frequent reporting on her activities helped spread use of the title outside Washington.

Many First Ladies have not liked the title "First Lady," but this has not stopped them from making their marks on history in diverse ways:

★ **Martha Washington,** the first First Lady, offered her silver service to use for the first coins minted in the United States.

★ **Abigail Smith Adams** and **Barbara Pierce Bush** are the only two women to have been both the wife of a president and the mother of another president. But Barbara Pierce Bush claims another distinction. She is also a descendant of Thomas Pierce, an ancestor of Franklin Pierce. Barbara Bush is a great-great-great-niece and a fourth cousin four times removed of President Pierce. Barbara Bush once quipped, "Somewhere out there in this audience may even be someone who will one day follow in my footsteps and preside over the White House as the president's spouse. I wish him well."

Barbara Pierce Bush

★ Often garbed in exotic gowns and turbans, **Dolley Paine Todd Madison** acted as the official hostess during Thomas Jefferson's administration as well as that of her husband. She was thus a President's House hostess for sixteen years, an accomplishment unmatched by any other woman in American history.

★ When British troops burned the White House in 1814, **Dolley Madison** courageously rescued Gilbert Stuart's famous portrait of George Washington before she fled the city. That most recognized of all presidential portraits is the only remaining possession from the original building.

Dolley Madison

★ **Martha Wayles Skelton Jefferson** and **Hannah Hoes Van Buren** both died eighteen years before their husbands were elected presidents of the United States. Daughter **Polly Jefferson Randolph** on occasion served as hostess at the White House, as did daughter-in-law **Angelica Singleton Van Buren.** In his autobiography, Van Buren never once mentions his wife.

★ In addition to being the wife of a president, **Anna Tuthill Symmes Harrison** holds a number of other distinctions. Because her husband, William Henry Harrison, lived for only thirty-one days as president, she didn't have enough time to join him in the White House. In addition to being First Lady for the shortest length of time, she is the oldest woman ever to become First Lady and the first to be widowed while holding the title. She is also the only First Lady to become the grandmother of a president, Benjamin Harrison.

Abigail Powers Fillmore

★ After the death of James Polk at the age of fifty-three, his widow, **Sarah Childress Polk,** dressed in mourning for the rest of her life.

★ Millard Fillmore was the only president to marry his schoolteacher, **Abigail Powers.** Two years younger than she, Fillmore was her student at New Hope Academy. Abigail was responsible for the installation of the first bathtub in the Executive Mansion, an act for which she incurred severe public criticism. Bathtubs have been a White House fixture ever since.

★ During the term of James Buchanan, our only bachelor president, his niece, **Harriet Lane,** played the role of First Lady.

Harriet Lane

★ Andrew Johnson married **Eliza McCardle** in 1827, when she was just seventeen years of age.

★ Rutherford B. and **Lucy Hayes** banned all forms of profanity, tobacco, and alcohol at presidential gatherings and functions. For this action the First Lady earned the nickname "Lemonade Lucy." A sideboard that had been presented to "Lemonade Lucy" Hayes by the Woman's Christian Temperance Union was purchased by a Washington saloonkeeper. He prominently displayed the sideboard in his barroom on Pennsylvania Avenue, loaded with liquors.

★ Like James Buchanan, Grover Cleveland entered the White House as a bachelor. At the age of forty-nine, President Cleveland married twenty-one-year-old **Frances Folsom** in the Blue Room of the White House. Frances became the youngest of all First Ladies, and the couple's baby, Esther, was the only child born in the White House to a president. When

Wedding of Grover Cleveland and Frances Folsom in White House, 1886

in 1889 her husband was voted out of office after his first term, Frances Folsom Cleveland told the staff to take care of the furniture because they would return. She was right.

★ First Lady **Caroline Harrison** is best known for her domestic successes. She modernized the White House, installing electricity in 1891 and electric kitchen appliances. She gained considerable attention when she designed the cornstalk-and-flower border for the china during her husband's administration, and she collected the china patterns of all her White House predecessors. Although her contemporaries gave more attention to her domestic accomplishments, she did far more. She agreed to fund-raise for the new Johns Hopkins University School of Medicine in 1890 on the grounds that women be admitted to study on the same basis as men, thus making one of the country's major medical schools coeducational.

Johns Hopkins Hospital

★ **Edith Kermit Carow Roosevelt,** First Lady at the turn of the last century, managed the White House while raising six children.

★ In 1912, **Helen Herron Taft,** popularly known as "Nellie," supervised the planting of the famous Washington cherry trees, a gift from the people of Tokyo.

★ **Edith Bolling Galt Wilson** has been called "the secret president" and "the first woman to run the government." This legend arose from her perceived role in affairs of state after Woodrow Wilson suffered a prolonged and debilitating illness. Edith was Woodrow's constant attendant and took over many routine duties of government. But she did not try to control the executive branch. In her 1939 *My Memoir,* she wrote: "So began my stewardship. I studied every paper, sent from the different Secretaries or senators, and tried to digest and present in tabloid form the things that, despite my vigilance, had to go to the President. I myself never made a single decision regarding the disposition of public affairs. The only decision that was mine was what was important and what was not, and

Cherry trees framing the Jefferson Memorial

the very important decision of when to present matters to my husband." Edith Wilson died on December 28, 1961, the anniversary of Woodrow's birth.

★ Like her husband, **Lou Henry Hoover** was also an engineer and happened to be fluent in Chinese. She was also national president of the Girl Scouts of the United States.

★ **(Anna) Eleanor Roosevelt** broke precedent to hold press conferences, travel to all parts of the country, give lectures and radio broadcasts, and express her opinions candidly in a daily syndicated newspaper column, "My Day."

★ When **Eleanor Roosevelt** informed Vice President Harry Truman that her husband, Franklin, had died, Truman asked, "Is there anything I can do for you?" Shaking her head, Mrs. Roosevelt said, "Is there anything we can do for you? For you are the one in trouble now."

Lou Hoover (center) with Girl Scouts, 1929

★ Being from the Midwest, President Harry Truman often talked to farm groups. Whenever he held forth about fertilizer, Truman used the word *manure,* much to the embarrassment of his support staff. Finally, the public relations people went to **Bess Truman** to ask her help in getting her husband to stop using the offending word. She sighed, "You'd be amazed how long it took me to get him to start using *manure.*"

★ On Valentine's Day, 1962, **Jacqueline Kennedy** offered a tour of the White

Jacqueline Kennedy

House on television. Three out of four viewers tuned into that program, the most watched documentary of television's golden age. For her hour-long broadcast, the National Academy of Television Arts and Sciences awarded her an honorary Emmy.

★ **Lady Bird Johnson** championed the planting of more than a million wildflowers to beautify the nation's highways. She has been called the first

conservationist to occupy the White House since Theodore Roosevelt.

★ When **Betty Ford** unexpectedly became First Lady after Richard Nixon resigned, she wrote, "I was an ordinary woman who was called onstage at an extraordinary time. I was no different once I became first lady than I had been before. But, through an accident of history, I had become interesting to people." She made history when she openly discussed her diagnosis and

Betty Ford wearing ERA button, 1975

treatment for breast cancer and helped raise public awareness of the disease.

★ **Hillary Rodham Clinton** is the first and only First Lady to be elected to high office, as senator from New York. She is also the first First Lady to have earned a law degree, from Yale Law School, where she met her future husband. In 1997 she won a Grammy Award for her spoken version of her book *It Takes a Village.* In 2009, she became secretary of state, and in 2016 became the first woman to be nominated for president by a major party.

★ **Michelle LaVaughn Robinson Obama** is the second First Lady to have earned a law degree, having studied at Harvard Law School, where she met her future husband. At the 2016 Democratic Convention in Philadelphia, she became the first First Lady to speak on behalf of a fellow First Lady running for president. Among her many causes, she championed exercise and healthy eating.

Eleanor Roosevelt

★ **Melania Trump** is the second foreign-born First Lady in American history, born in Novo Mesto, in what is now Slovenia. The first was John Quincy Adams's wife, **Louisa Adams,** who was born in England. At 5 feet 11 inches, **Eleanor Roosevelt, Michelle Obama,** and **Melania Trump** are the loftiest of our First Ladies.

Here, **alphabetically** by first name, are listed the names of sixteen first ladies before they hooked up with presidents. Identify each president to whom they were married.

1. Claudia (Lady Bird) Taylor
2. Elizabeth (Betty) Bloomer
3. Ellen Louise Axson
4. Elizabeth Kortright
5. Elizabeth Virginia (Bess) Wallace
6. Jacqueline Lee (Jackie) Bouvier
7. Julia Dent
8. Julia Gardiner
9. Laura Welch
10. Letitia Christian
11. Lou Henry
12. Mamie Geneva Doud
13. Mary Paine Todd
14. Nancy Davis
15. Thelma Catherine (Pat) Ryan
16. Rosalynn Smith

ANSWERS

1. Lyndon Johnson
2. Gerald Ford
3. Woodrow Wilson
4. James Monroe
5. Harry Truman
6. John F. Kennedy
7. Ulysses S. Grant
8. John Tyler
9. George W. Bush
10. John Tyler
11. Herbert Hoover
12. Dwight Eisenhower
13. Abraham Lincoln
14. Ronald Reagan
15. Richard Nixon
16. Jimmy Carter

A PRIMER OF
POLITICAL
WORDS

★ ★ ★ ★

Biennial departure of "lame duck" members of Congress

AS OUR PRESIDENTIAL campaigns become increasingly feverish, frenetic, fervent, frantic, and frenzied, we understand why in England people *stand* for election, but in the United States they *run*. It's also a time that demonstrates that although the classical societies of ancient Greece and Rome have vanished, Greek and Roman thought are very much alive in the parlance of politics.

Taking first things first, let's start with the word *primary*, which descends from the Latin *primus*, "first." *Primary*, as a shortening of "primary election," is first recorded in 1861. In an *election* we "pick out" a candidate who we wish to vote for. In Latin *e* means "out" and *lectus* "pick or choose."

As the joke goes, the etymology of the word *politics* derives from *poly*, which means "many," and *tics*, which are blood-sucking parasites. In truth, *politics* issues from the Greek word *polites*, "city, citizen." Politics may make strange bedfellows, but as you'll soon see, politics makes for even stranger, and sometimes colorful, vocabulary.

Campaign is very much a fighting word. The Latin *campus*, "field," is a clue that the first campaigns were conducted on battlefields. A military campaign is a series of operations mounted to achieve a particular wartime objective. A political campaign is an all-out effort to secure the election of a candidate to office.

The Battle of Munfordville, 1862

When he went to the Forum in Roman times, a candidate for office wore a bleached white toga to symbolize his humility, purity of motive, and candor. The original Latin root, *candidatus*, meant "one who wears white," from the belief that white was the color of purity and probity. There was wishful thinking even in ancient Roman politics, even though a white-clad Roman *candidatus* was accompanied by *sectatores,* followers who helped him get votes by bargaining and bribery. The Latin parent verb *candere,* "to shine, to glow," can be recognized in the English words *candid, candor, candle,* and *incandescent.*

We know that candidates are ambitious. It's also worth knowing that *ambition* developed from the Latin *ambitionem,* "a going about," from the going about of candidates for office in ancient Rome.

President descends from the Latin *praesidio,* "preside, sit in front of, or protect." Presidents sit in the seat of government. When we speak of "the ship of state," we are being more accurate etymologically than we know. The Greek word *kybernao* meant "to direct a ship." The Romans borrowed the word as *guberno,* and ultimately it crossed the English Channel as *governor,* originally a steersman. That's why the noun is *governor* and the adjective *gubernatorial.*

The vote that we cast is really a "vow" or "wish." And this is the precise meaning of the Latin *votum.* People in our society who fail to exercise their democratic privilege of voting on Election Day are sometimes called idiots.

The original Greek meaning of the word *idiot* was not nearly as harsh as our modern sense. Long before the psychologists got ahold of the word, the Greeks used *idiotes,* from the root *idios,* "private," as in *idiom* and *idiosyncrasy,* to designate those who did not hold public office. Because such people possessed no special status or skill, the word *idiot* gradually fell into disrepute.

A metaphor (the word originally meant "to carry across" in Greek) is a figure of speech that merges two seemingly different objects or ideas. We usually think of metaphors as figurative devices that only poets create, but in fact all of us make metaphors during almost every moment of our waking lives. As T. E. Hulme observed, "Prose is a museum, where all the old weapons of poetry are kept."

Take the political expression "to throw one's hat in the ring." The phrase probably derives from the custom of tossing one's hat into the boxing ring to signal the acceptance of a pugilist's challenge. Once the hat is thrown, the candidates start engaging in political infighting as they slug it out with their opponents.

Or take the expression "to carry the torch for someone." During the nineteenth century, a dedicated follower showed support for a political candidate by carrying a torch in an evening campaign parade. A fellow who carried a torch in such a rally didn't care who knew that he was wholeheartedly behind his candidate. Later the term was applied to someone publicly (and obsessively) in love.

To take one more metaphor that was originally literal, bandwagons were high wagons large enough to hold a band of musicians. Early bandwagons were horse drawn through the streets in order to publicize an upcoming event. Political candidates would ride a bandwagon through a town, and those who wished to show their support would hop (or climb) onto the bandwagon and ride with the candidate and his blaring band.

Horses and horse racing are dominant animal metaphors that gallop through political life. One of the earliest of equine metaphors is "dark horse." The figure refers to a political candidate who is nominated unexpectedly, usually as a result of compromise between two factions in a party. Dark-horse candidates who became president include **James Polk** in 1844, **Franklin Pierce** in 1852, **Rutherford B. Hayes** in 1876, **James Garfield** in 1880, and **Warren Harding** in 1920.

Presidents have running mates. This too is a horse-racing term and derives from the practice of one owner or one stable running two horses in a race, the slower one being put in there to pace the star. The pacesetter was known as the star's running mate. The phrase has been around for more than a century, but its use to define a vice president was coined by, of all nonpractitioners of slang, the most scholarly, the most ecclesiastical of presidents, **Woodrow Wilson.** At the Democratic Convention in 1912, the presidential nomination went to Wilson on the forty-sixth ballot after a terrific brawl. Governor Wilson of New Jersey announced that his vice presidential choice would be another governor, Thomas Marshall, and announced, "And I feel honored by having him as my running mate." Wilson's turn of phrase brought the house down, the

only squeak of humor those assembled had ever heard out of President Wilson.

Presidential jockeying for position gets out of the gate earlier and earlier with each campaign. It remains to be seen whether the next presidential contest will turn out to be a runaway or a real horse race. Will a dark horse give the frontrunner a run for his or her money? Will the old warhorse and his or her running mate, saddled with international and economic problems, turn out to be shoo-ins or lame ducks?

IMAGE CREDITS

Page 9: EH/SS
Page 10: U.S. Post Office/WM
Pages 11–12: EH/SS
Page 13: ra3rn/SS
Page 14: Stocksnapper/SS
Page 16 (Wilson): EH/SS
Page 16 (woman voter): LC (LC-DIG-ggbain-08785)
Page 18: Frank Turgeon Jr./WM
Page 19: catwalker/SS
Page 20: Bob McNeely (WH)/WM
Page 21: LC (LC-DIG-ppmsca-23683)
Pages 23–29: EH/SS
Page 30: WH/WM
Page 31: Cecil Stoughton/WM
Page 32: MC/SS
Page 34: Eric Draper (WH)/WM
Page 35: LC (LC-DIG-ppmsca-35735)
Page 37: Mathew Brady/WM
Page 38: LC (LC-USZ62-16960)
Page 39: EH/SS
Page 40: © Moffett, Chicago (J241772, U.S. Copyright Office)/WM
Page 41: Elias Goldensky/WM
Page 42: WM
Page 43: S.Sgt. Lono Kollars/WM
Page 46: WM
Page 47 (Harvard): MC/SS
Page 47 (Obama): Pete Souza (WH)/WM
Page 48: LC (LC-USZ62-100027)
Page 50: EH/SS
Page 52: Daniel M. Silva/SS
Page 53: LC (LC-USZC4-3616)
Page 54: The Graphic Co./WM
Page 55: © Richard K. Fox, New York (photo by Chickering, Boston)/WM
Page 56: FDR Presidential Library & Museum (photo by Margaret Suckley)/WM
Page 57: Courtesy Ronald Reagan Library/WM
Page 59: LC (LC-USZ62-100816)
Page 60: Smithsonian Museum of Natural History/WM

Page 61: LC (LC-USZ6-627)
Page 63: David Hume Kennerly/WM
Page 64: Marion anthrax/WM
Page 66: Department of the Navy, Naval Photographic Center/WM
Page 68: Harris & Ewing/WM
Page 69: LC (LC-DIG-ppmsca-23851)
Pages 70–75: EH/SS
Pages 76–77: WM
Page 79: UKRID/SS
Page 80: LC (LC-USZ62-112163)
Page 81: © Charles Scribner's Sons/ LC (LC-USZ62-101366)
Page 83: G. Frank E. Pearsall/WM
Page 84: LC (LC-USZ62-48103)/WM
Page 85: LC (LC-DIG-pga-00724)
Pages 86–87: WM
Page 89: U.S. National Archives and Records Administration/WM
Page 90: WM
Page 91: Abbie Rowe/WM
Page 92: Associated Press/WM
Page 93: LC (LC-DIG-pga-01447)
Page 94: Goudey/WM
Page 96: © A. H. Ritchie/ LC (LC-USZ62-71730)
Page 97: EH/SS
Page 98: Alexander Gardner/WM
Page 100: LC, Theodor Horydczak Collection (LC-H812-T-M09-004-A)
Page 101: Ollie Atkins (WH)/WM
Page 102: Internet Archive Book Images/WM
Page 103: Unique Multiples/WM
Page 104: EH/SS
Page 106: LC (LC-DIG-ds-04676)
Page 107: LC (LC-DIG-ppmsca-09761)
Page 109: Mathew Brady/WM
Page 110: Courtesy of the General Libraries, University of Texas at Austin/WM
Page 111: Cecil W. Stoughton/WM
Page 112: Record Group 111, Records of the Office of the Chief Signal Officer (111-SC-578830)/WM

Page 113: EH/SS
Page 114: WH/WM
Page 116: Michael Vadon/WM
Page 117: LC (LC-USZ62-24155)
Page 118: Courtesy of the General Libraries, University of Texas at Austin/WM
Page 119: Ollie Atkins (WH)/WM
Page 120: Nelson E. Baldwin (Historic American Buildings Survey)/WM
Page 122: Edmonston Studio/WM
Page 124: EH/SS
Page 126: S. Chua/WM
Page 127: U.S. Senate/WM
Page 128: EH/SS
Page 129: LC (LC-H2- B-8960)
Page 131: From a painting by J. Mund/WM
Page 132: LC (LC-USZ62-76296)
Page 133 (Dawes): LC (LC-USZ6-849)
Page 133 (Curtis): EH/SS
Page 135 (Stevenson): Napoleon Sarony/WM
Page 135 (Rockefeller): WH/WM
Page 136: LC (LC-DIG-pga-04936)
Page 138 (Bush): Bush Presidential Library/WM
Page 138 (Madison): WM
Pages 139–40: WM
Page 141: EH/SS
Page 142 (Johns Hopkins): Wellcome Images/WM
Page 142 (cherry trees): Anita Mishra/WM
Page 143: LC (LC-F8- 42781)
Page 144 (Kennedy): LC (LC-USZ62-25815)
Page 144 (Ford): WH/WM
Page 145: WM
Page 147: Clifford K. Berryman/WM
Page 148: EH/SS
Page 150: Everett Collection/SS
Page 151: Wellcome Images/WM